Some Thoughts For The Journey To Cana

Christian Matrimony
Choice
or
Chance?

by

Pastor Michael S. Williams, D.Min

Resource *Publications*
An imprint of *Wipf and Stock Publishers*
199 West 8th Avenue • Eugene OR 97401

Resource *Publications*
an imprint of Wipf and Stock Publishers
199 West 8th Avenue, Suite 3
Eugene, Oregon 97401

Some Thoughts For The Journey To Cana
Christian Matrimony, Choice or Chance
By Williams, Michael S.
©2001 Williams, Michael S.
ISBN: 1-57910-805-9
Publication date: November, 2001
Previously published by , 2001.

1

TABLE OF CONTENTS

Introduction 3

Marriage: Myth, Reality, And The Bible 35

Marriage: Religious Differences, To Yoke Or Not To Yoke—That Is The Question! Can Saved And Unsaved People Marry? 52

Marriage: Finances—The Straw That Can Break Your Marital Back! 64

Marriage And Family Relationships: "Excuse Me—Point Of Clarification Here, Am I Marrying You Or Your Mother?" 81

Marriage: Emotional And Physical Health: Do You Want A Spouse Or A "Patient"? 92

Marriage: Professional And Vocational Goals—"Hey, What About Me?" 110

Epilogue 123

Introduction

This volume, *Some Thoughts for the Journey to Cana: Christian Matrimony, Choice or Chance?* arises from nearly three decades of ministry. I have presided over scores of weddings since my ordination in 1979. However, I must confess, many of those marriages have not lasted. Some have *lasted*, but in many cases the couples are merely going through the motions.

As I reflected upon the success/failure ratio of those marriages, I found that what passed for "pre-marital counseling" was merely sitting with the engaged couple for about an hour and going over their wedding plans! I don't think I'm alone in this; with domestic violence and divorce rates literally sky rocketing, ordained Christian clergy share a great deal of the blame for affording couples shaky foundations, in place of the rock solid Word of God upon which to build their lives together!

I believe—and I stand to be corrected—that slip-shod pre-marital counseling on the part of clergy is an occupational hazard. One reason could be due to our seminary curriculum. A cursory glance at current seminary course offerings will betray a heavy dose of Biblical studies, Church history, Ethics, denominational polity, and worship studies. However,

when it comes to pastoral care within the context of parish ministry, the offerings are slim to none.
I was at a loss as to how to address this problem. Seminary didn't prepare me. "On-the-Job-Training" certainly didn't! Listening to "war stories" coming from "seasoned" colleagues perhaps did more harm than good.
In 1996, the Lord brought about a revolution in my thinking. Actually, two occurrences began to pull me in the direction that finally culminated in this book. First, one day, while driving down the freeway from my home in San Francisco, California, towards the city of San Jose, I listened to the early morning broadcast of the news on my car radio. The radio was tuned to National Public Radio's local affiliate, KQED 88.5 FM. That morning, NPR did an in-depth story on a program initiated by an interdenominational group of pastors in the city of Modesto, California. It seemed as if they were experiencing problems similar to mine. They resolved to do something about it. In 1986, they entered into covenant with each other not to preside over any wedding unless the couple agreed to involve themselves in an intensive, as well as extensive, four month pre-marital counseling program. The original ninety-five participants formulated and agreed upon what would later become the *Community Marriage Policy*. This was the first of its type in the nation!
The course is pretty tough, as well as non-conventional. Among other things, couples are required to go through a battery of psychological tests so as to understand each other's temperament. Sessions are also held that deal with such hot topics as financial management for couples, and the Biblical nature of marriage. I guess *love* was somewhere to be found within the curriculum, but it played a very minor role. None

of that "dewey eyed," romantic stuff claimed central stage. Of course, love and romance come into the process; but the couples are taught that weddings can last about fifteen to twenty minutes, but marriages are meant to last a lifetime! Through the implementation of this program, the pastors were able to see an observable decline in troubled marriages and divorces in the Greater Modesto area!

The second step in my discovery process occurred in 1997 when I presided over a wedding. Including me, there were to be three preachers involved. I was to lead in the recitation of the vows. My two colleagues were to do a short homily and prayer, respectively. The preacher assigned to do the homily was not able to attend, so at the last minute, rather than cause pandemonium within the wedding party, I did the homily. Little did I know that the Lord put me in that position to show me a thing or two about marriage. I thought and thought. Nothing seemed to come to mind. Sometimes I have trouble thinking on my feet, but it just so happened the Lord gave me the right things to say. Suddenly, the story about Jesus turning water into wine at Cana (**John 2:1-11**) entered my consciousness.

While I can't remember what I said verbatim, I can remember my homily in "the rough". I related to the couple that in Biblical times, weddings did not consist of thirty-minute ceremonies. They could, in many cases, go on for days at a time. In fact, the Bible seems to infer that a wedding could last up to a week (**Genesis 29:27-28**)!

The wedding ceremony encompassed a celebratory feast at one of the parents' homes. Weddings were very elaborate affairs; the guest list was carefully drawn up (**Matthew**

22:3).[1] It was considered an insult to turn the invitation down (**Matthew 22:5**). When it came to the actual wedding feast, no expense was to be spared (**Matthew 22:4**). Also, it seems that seating arrangements were very important; *who* sat *where* was rigidly controlled. To sit in the wrong place could cause offense, and have the offender publicly embarrassed (**Luke 14: 7-10**). The Bible seems to imply that special garments were to be worn by the guests. To be improperly dressed could get guests in trouble with the host (**Matthew 22:11-13**).

The custom of the day dictated when you had guests, regardless of the occasion—whether expected or not. As host, you were duty bound to make sure that nothing was amiss (**Genesis 18: 1-8**). First, your guest's comfort was a matter of personal honor. To disregard your guest's comfort was a major sign of disrespect (**Luke 7:44-47**). To *run out* of food or drink was considered a disgrace.

At Cana, a crisis occurred; the wine ran out (**John 2:2**)! But as I related to the couple, the host was wise enough to have invited Jesus to the wedding. I told them that, with the Master in attendance, whatever shortfalls may occur, they could be made up with just a Word from Him!

Sure enough, the host had tried to prepare for his guests, but even with the best of preparation, he still ran short of wine! Second, notice that Jesus' mother had the presence of

---

[1] According to M. Eugene Boring, during New Testament times, Rabbinical, as well as Hellenistic (Greek), custom dictated that two invitations went out to alert the wedding guests concerning the actual event. The first invitation went out well in advance of the actual wedding. The second invitation served as a reminder of the wedding. It went out the day festivities were set to begin. M. Eugene Boring, "The Gospel of Matthew: Introduction, Commentary, and Reflections," ed. Leander E. Keck, et.al, *The Interpreter's Bible,* vol. 9 (Abingdon Press, 1995), 417.

mind to call on the Master! Mary was Jesus' *mother*, but she also realized that He was her *Lord* (**John 2:3**)! This is very important to understand! Within the context of Christian fellowship, the only relationships that our Master holds to be ultimately important are those rooted in His Will! This may be a hard pill to swallow, but to the Master, *even our family ties* and *close relationships* must be *secondary* to our fellowship with Him (**Matthew 10:34-39, 12: 46-50**). Jesus turned the water into wine and literally saved the day (**John 2:7-10**).

My point to the couple was this: no matter what *we* bring to our marital table, *we* will *run out*! I told them that no matter how much:

- "lovey-dovey,"
- romance,
- sex,
- money,
- tolerance,
- good intentions,
- promises,
- and good will,

the two of them would bring to the marital table, in the end their provisions *would run out*!

So What's The Point Of This Book?

Actually, I have two!

- The first point demands that we soberly ask ourselves, in light of our Christian experience as well as the Biblical witness, some tough questions. We must ask ourselves: What do we bring to the marital table? Are the provisions adequate? Are they fresh? Have they spoiled? Are they obsolete? Are they *Biblically* based?

- Second, before we begin the journey to our "Cana," will we find the Master waiting there? Ask yourself, has He been invited? Or better yet, has He instructed *you* to go there?

As we build upon the foundation laid before us above, it means we must seek His Will for our married life. How can we ascertain His Will? The chief aim of this book, in concert with the Bible, is to assist you in discerning the Lord's Will for your life in reference to marriage.

Some Thoughts for the Journey to Cana: Christian Matrimony: Choice or Chance? will give you the opportunity to reflect upon your marriage plans and ask, "Is marriage *at this*:
- particular time, *to this*
- particular person, *at this*
- particular moment in my life's journey—*God's Will* for me?"

Now, It's Time To Ask Yourself:

Who Says I Can't "Blow It" Or Even Derail My Life By Marrying Someone In Direct Violation To The Will Of God For My Life?

Just as the host at the wedding in Cana faced private—and even worse public—humiliation, to enter into a union that has not been endorsed by our Master will cause the same thing—an embarrassing situation that may take *years* to unravel—*if it can* **ever be** *unraveled*. No, I didn't make a typo, I *meant* to put *"ever be"* in bold letters, because **I WANT YOU TO KNOW THAT UNRAVELLING THE TANGLED AND MANGLED REMNANTS OF YOUR LIFE CAUSED BY A FOOLISH MARRIAGE DECISION CAN TAKE YEARS TO ACCOMPLISH. BUT, ON THE OTHER HAND, GOD MAY NEVER LET YOU "OFF THE HOOK"; YOU MAY HAVE TO PAY FOR YOUR DECISION FOR THE REST OF YOUR LIFE!** Why would He do such a thing? Because, according to **Hebrews 12:5-11**, He loves us enough to teach us hard lessons).

A marriage that is unsanctioned by the Lord will trap you in a marital furnace. Even if the Lord sanctions your marriage, *He* must be called upon to replenish whatever runs out! An unsanctioned marriage will make you desert the Will of the Father, the Lordship of Christ, and the power of the Holy Spirit, and resort to worldly notions that counsel us that it's "cheaper to keep her (or him)".

Now You Can Understand Why I Gave This Book Such A Peculiar Title!

In order to give you fair warning concerning the pitfalls of an unholy union, I've entitled this book, *Some Thoughts For The Journey To Cana: Christian Matrimony, Choice Or Chance?* When it comes to marriage, you will either make an intelligent *choice*, arising out the Will of the Lord, or take a foolish *chance*—a **gamble** if you will—that things will all work out by themselves.

Within the Christian life, there is no such thing as gambling or wishing. Either we are in the Perfect Will of God, or we are not! And remember a *marital gamble* is no different than a game of *chance* such as poker, the lottery, slot machines, keno, or bingo. You *may* win, but the odds are stacked against you, and it stands to experience that you *will* lose. And when you lose, depending upon whom you owe, you can forfeit a great deal of your blessings! Remember, the minute you step into a casino—as any seasoned gambler will tell you—"The house will always wins!" This means that you are automatically a loser once you put your money into a slot machine. If that were the case with gambling, *why would you*

enter into a marriage on that basis? The moment you've entered in without the Lord's permission, you have lost! No matter how much
- Sex,
- Money,
- Property you own,
- Gifts you buy each other,
- Children or,
- How long you've known each other, or
- You've "lived together" (Which is kinda silly anyway! Why should s/he "buy the cow, when s/he can get the milk for free?"), or
- Social activities,

you place into the slot machine of your relationship, you *will* walk away **broke** (or even worse—mentally, physically, spiritually, financially or professionally **broken**)!

12

If you enter into an ungodly marital situation, not only will you end up "broke," but broken! I know, I know—you're saying, "I'm different, it won't happen to me," but what makes you so special? Stronger people than you have been "broken!"

You may think that you are smarter than the average person and that you can handle anything—but look my friend, when you gamble, Satan is the dealer, and he always uses "loaded dice." When you gamble with a crooked pair of dice, you always **LOSE**. Before you journey to Cana, ask yourself, "How much can I afford to **LOSE**?"

- Can I afford to *lose* my mind?
- Can I afford to *lose* my retirement account?
- Can I afford to *destroy* in a few short months what took years to build?
- Can I afford to *lose* my self-respect?
- Can I afford to have my self-esteem *battered*?
- Can I afford to allow my anger to well up after I realize my mistake and then hurt myself or even *kill* or *injure* my spouse in a fit of rage?

If you marry outside of the Will of God, you *will* surely find out that you made a huge mistake. You may then decide that a divorce would be much too costly and embarrassing; the next step could be to "go under cover" and obey the ethic that tells us that,

> "Me-*yaaaaaaaaand* Mrs. Jones, Mrs. Jones, Mrs. Jones, (or Mr.) Jones, we have a *thingggggh* going on! We both know that it's wrong, but it's much to strong to let it go now!"

That is why it's important to make sure that the Master sanctions our marriages. He *will not*, and indeed *cannot*, if He has not been invited! And even if He is invited, we have to be sure that He wants to come! That is where obedience to *His* Will enters in!

How can it be ascertained that it is the Master's Will that the "two" of you should "become one"? The more I reflect upon that question, the more I think it has something to do with the quality of our relationship with God, through Jesus Christ. This involves following the Master. To follow Him means we are obedient to His Word and His Call. An excellent model of this is found in the Gospels. The disciple enters into a relationship with Jesus through a *call* (**Matthew 4:18-22**). The Master then *teaches* the disciple (**Matthew 5:1-2**). The call and teaching aspects of the Christian's *followship* has a direct bearing on the Christian's quality of life. A high quality relationship with Jesus that involves *following* Him, will allow you to *fellowship* with others. If you *follow* Jesus, then you will not have a problem *fellowshipping* with a spouse! In other words, the quality of our *marital* relationship has a direct connection to the quality of our *relationship* with the Master. As a Christian, whether you want to admit it or not, it's impossible to love someone else, unless you are in love with our Master *first* (**1 John 2:1-11**). If we don't take Him seriously, then our lives and relationships will show it!

Jesus, the "Word made Flesh," through the Bible, provides *the* solid foundation for marriage. To use anything other than His Word is to court disaster (**Matthew 7:24-27**). This dictates that we follow Him and literally devour every word that spills from His Blessed lips! A *call* to *follow* means that we are to *learn* from *and* of *Him*. (**Matthew 11:28-30**)!

This is why the Disciples, as foolish as they were at times, were always in a learning mode when it came to our Master (**Mark 4:10, 33-34, Luke 11:1**)!

So many times, Christian life—and Christian matrimony is no exception—flounders because it has been entered into ignoring the Word of God. For instance, though the question of marriage was not directly involved, I would suggest that, God through our Lord Jesus, was on target when He admonished His followers to "count up the cost" and to give serious consideration prior to making any serious commitment (**Luke 14:28-33**). In that context, Jesus spoke explicitly about the cost of being a disciple of His. If following Jesus entails such serious thought, *how much more thought can matrimonial union with another person be*? This is why the Psalmist compared the Word of God to a "lamp unto his feet and a light unto his path"(**Psalms 119: 105**). The Psalmist infers that God's word must be ingested so as to be drawn upon when necessary (**Psalms 119:11**). It's when we take the Word to heart that we are kept from grievous errors! In other words in order to keep from the paths of destruction, Christians should scrutinize all serious decisions, *especially marriage*, prior to hastily "leaping in." And this *close scrutiny* must be done in light of the Word of God! Why? Because the Bible is our rule of Faith! It is, as my Old Testament professor, John Otwell of Berkeley, California's world-renowned Pacific School of Religion, now of blessed memory once said, "God's gift to the church."

I Hate To Destroy Your Illusions, But No Matter How Many Times You Kiss Your Frog, S/he Will Remain Just That—Reptilian. If You Discount The Will Of Our Master And Actually "Become One" With Your "Prince/ss," You Will Begin To Look A Little "Green Around The Gills" Yourself!

For the Christian, a life lived uninformed by the Scriptures is a guaranteed disaster! The Bible is not just "another book," it is *God's* Book (**2 Timothy 3:14-16, 2 Peter 1:12-21**).

When one "leaps" into an ill-advised marriage, one can fairly expect to say "I do!" on the day of the wedding and wake up three months later, and ask his/herself, "I did?" There can be no greater letdown than finding out that your "Prince" (or "Princess") Charming is nothing more than a toad. But unlike the fairy tale, no matter how many times you kiss that person, s/he will remain reptilian. If you stick around that person long enough, you'll begin to look a bit green around the gills yourself! For this cause, as the Master's Disciples, as we gather together for fellowship, one of the main purposes is to *learn* how to discern our Master's Will and Desires concerning our life's course (**Matthew 11:28-29**).

This means laying *aside* pride, personal inclinations, as well as family traditions, and reflecting upon these "lay *asides*" in light of the Word of God. This is what, in part, the writer of Hebrews meant when he counseled us to "lay aside" everything that would entangle us, and concentrate on our Divine focal point—Jesus (**Hebrews 12:1-2**).

God's Word Is A Lamp Shining Before Our Feet. It Sheds Light Upon Our Pathway (Psalms 119:105).

This means, as Dr. Willie Richardson, pastor of Philadelphia's Christian Stronghold Baptist Church, admonishes us, the local church *must* become a Family Training Center. He believes—and I concur wholeheartedly—that quality marriages *do not* automatically fall into place; we have to *learn* how to be spouses![2] But tragically, couples enter into marital relationships with immature, half-baked ideas concerning what makes for a successful marriage. Some couples think that just because:

- Their fornicating (engaging in pre-marital sex) is "da bomb," everything will work out ok. (Hey, hate to burst your bubble, but even sex gets old. Besides, can you handle the other aspects of their personality? A person can be an excellent sex partner and a very silly person simultaneously!)

- You were married previously (Oh yeah, this time is the right time! Think about it though! You could be making the same mistake all over again!). If you think that's true, check out **Proverbs 26:11**!

---

[2] Dr. Richardson makes several excellent suggestions concerning pre-marital counseling. He points out the following areas of emphasis: First, families should not be left on their own without help. Second, single people must be *prepared* for marriage. Third, married couples need to be *trained*. Fourth, teenaged children need to be *taught* about marriage. Dr. Willie Richardson, *Reclaiming the Urban Family: How to Mobilize the Church as a Family Training Center* (Grand Rapids, MI: ZondervanPublishingHouse, 1996), 25-31.

- Your future spouse happens to be older than you—that his/her foolish years are over (Why would you *think* that just because a person is *older than you* that they are mature? S/he can be several years older than you and still be foolish and irresponsible. The fact that s/he is older than you means that s/he could've had a longer period of time to get set in their childish and destructive ways).[3]

- Or are marrying a younger person that they can mold that person's character. (All younger persons are teachable, right? Wake up! You are dreaming—hey, what have you been drinking? If you go by that, then watch what happens when you get married; maybe that person *is* teachable—but you won't have a marriage, you will have a kindergarten. To this I would say, if that were the case, why don't you consider adoption?)[4]

An Alternative to Just "Leaping In"

Whoa! Put the brakes on! Before you go rushing to the county clerk's office with your $25.00 and blood tests in hand, listen to the Master! The Master tells us that we are to be as "wise as *snakes*, but as harmless as *doves"* (**Matthew**

---

[3] While there is nothing inherently wrong with so-called "May-December" unions, recent research findings inform us that they carry within them certain risks peculiar to those types of relationships, especially if they advance to the matrimonial stage. Frank Pittman, MD, "Beware Older Women Ahead," Psychology Today, January/February 1999, 60.

[4] Ibid.

10:16). In the ancient world, the snake was regarded as clever and cautious (**Genesis 3:1**); the dove was a symbol of the Holy Spirit (**Matthew 3:16**). The dove also symbolized safety and peace (**Genesis 8: 6-12**). A fruitful life in Christ dictates that we combine wisdom and the informative power of the Holy Spirit.

A person functioning solely with wisdom can become corrupt and cynical. A person just going by what is thought to be the "Spirit" is dangerous! Both wisdom and the Holy Spirit must combine in order make for a fruitful life! To put it another way, being a Christian doesn't mean that you park your Godly wisdom *or* anointing at the door prior to going before a judge or minister to get married. Before you get to that stage, you need to be in dialogue with *both*! That's why the Master tells us to be both wise *and* filled with the Holy Spirit. Without wisdom, you will mistake a *feeling* or an *urge* for the Holy Spirit. Without the Holy Spirit, you may be *wise*, but *cold* and *calculating*.

Remember, The Master Admonishes us to be As "Wise As Serpents, But….

...As Humble As Doves" (Matthew 10:16).

You may object at this point and accuse me of trying to "stifle" love. Listen, you don't know what *stifling* is until you have entered a marriage that *is not ordained by God*! If there is such a thing as a "living hell," it could be likened to a marriage that is *not* of God's making.

This book suggests that it's wise to look at *all* of the "angles" prior to walking down the aisle. I've advised the membership of the Saint James Missionary Baptist Church that I *will not* perform *any* wedding ceremony where the couple has not gone through the pre-marital process outlined in this book. So as to pre-empt any cries of:

1. Does that mean we can't get married?

2. Who are *you* to judge whether *we* can get married or not?

3. Well, we'll just have to take this *before the church*!

4. My family has belonged to this church for decades, who do you think you are?

5. You had better do as we say; after all, *we pay you*!

6. Does that mean we can't use the church?

7. Well—you sure are cold!

8. I thought you were a *preacher*!

9. But the invitations have been sent out!

HERE ARE MY ANSWERS

1) No, it does not mean *you* cannot get *married*; it's just that *I will not* perform the ceremony. You may still get married; however, you will have to get someone else to perform the ceremony. There are lots of religious leaders, judges, and functionaries both here and in Nevada's "wedding chapel" industry that would just love to take your money in exchange for you making the biggest mistake of your life.

2) On the contrary, I am not judging as to whether *you* can get married; it's just that *I* will not be a party to it.

3) Take it before the church; it's your right! I will give *them* the same answer I gave *you*.

4) I'm glad you have roots in the church. That's quite commendable!

5) Money is not the controlling factor in my life—the love of God is. Money doesn't make *me; I* make money. I'm not very good at serving two Masters. I've tried it, and believe-you-me; it *never* works (**Matthew 6:24, Acts 8: 18:20, 1 Timothy 6:10**).

6) In order to use the church, all you have to do is to contact the trustees and make the arrangements. They will be happy to accommodate you.

7) Well, all I can say is, "Sticks and stones..."

8) I *am* a *preacher*; what's more, I'm a *pastor*. My most important duty within the life of this fellowship is pastoral care (**Acts 6:2, 20: 28-29 Ephesians 4:11-12, Hebrews 13:17**).

9) I refer you back to the answer I gave you to question number six. *I just won't be there.* There are several things I have thankfully missed in my life:

- I've never witnessed an autopsy

- I registered for the draft, but was never "called up" for duty in Vietnam, so I missed the carnage of battle (all of the combat veterans I know tell me I did not miss much)!

- I've never witnessed a natural or man-made disaster— I've heard such sights are pretty gruesome!

Since I've never witnessed any of those things, I'd just as soon miss you going down the aisle and having the Holy Spirit whisper to me, "Dead man/woman walking!" The church can be available to you, but I'll probably take my wife to the movies, catch up on some studying, or go home and spend the rest of the day goofing off.

The Purpose of This Book Is To Serve As...

- ...a screening tool for those of you that are *contemplating* marriage.

- ...a reflection tool for those of you that may be *married*, *divorced*, or in the process of *obtaining a divorce*.

Its Purpose Is Definitely Not To...

...."Lay a trip" on anyone. If it's not God's Will for you to be in your current situation (i.e., engaged, divorced, in the process of divorcing, or married), rest assured my friend that *you* have "laid a trip" upon *yourself*! Don't take my word for it; just ask, those two dysfunctional parents of ours, Adam and Eve (**Genesis 3**)!

What this book describes is a *process*. This process has been put together for the purpose of letting you give the all-important act of marriage some serious *thought*. The late Dr. L.S. Ruben, organizing pastor of the Olivet Missionary Baptist Church of San Francisco's predominantly African-American Bayview/Hunters Point area, had a sign hanging from his pulpit. It consisted of one word—*THINK*. All too many times we Christians glory in what we *don't know*. We think of it as a badge of honor to go into any task without preparation. In other words, we just don't want to *THINK*! The great 19th Century African Methodist Episcopal Church Bishop, Daniel Payne described how this attitude was prevalent in the churches of his day. Pitifully so, it's still common in our day. It brags that favor with God equals a lack of training and understanding. Payne implies that there was a tacit understanding between the preacher and the congregation that conspired to keep each other as uninformed as possible! Says Payne,

> "...it was a common thing for preachers...to introduce their sermons by declaring that they had 'not rubbed their heads against college-walls,' at which the people would cry, '*Amen!*' [The preacher would then say, 'I've] never studied Latin or Greek,' at which the people would exclaim, '*Glory to God!*' [The preacher would then say, 'I've] never studied Hebrew,' at which all would *shout*."[5]

At The Risk Of Being Redundant, Let Me Just Say...

The basic aim of this book, especially in light of Bishop Payne's observations, is to provide a framework for intelligent as well as informed discussion on the part of Christian clergy and Christians[6] in *general*, but is for those

---

[5] Bishop Daniel Alexander Payne, *Recollections of Seventy Years* (New York: Arno Press and the New York Times, 1968), 64.

[6] Allow me to explain myself. I believe that a horrendous amount of blood has been spilled all in the name of defending religious faith. Our own century can bear witness to this! There is nothing more dangerous than a religious zealot that feels that it's permissible to maim, kill, and destroy all in the name of their faith tradition. However, I do not think of my self as being "religious." I unashamedly agree with the ancient hymn of the early church that claims that God has bestowed upon Jesus Christ a name that is above all other names. The Bible teaches us that at the name of Jesus, all knees must eventually bow and in turn all tongues must confess that He is Lord (**Philippians 2:9-11**). For that reason I never acknowledge that "we are all worshiping the same God."

Christians that may be contemplating marriage in *particular*. I know some of you are under the influence of that song from the 1960s that taught you, "all we need is love." That's what the song says, but God says, "In all of your getting, (that includes love and marriage)—get an understanding" (**Proverbs 4:7**). Notice I referenced *Christian* couples as the target for this discussion. I make no apologies for my *Christian* bias. Jesus of Nazareth is, for me, the Church's Risen Lord. Jesus of Nazareth is God's *final* revelation to the human family. He is not "one among many"—He is the *only* way to God (**Philippians 2:5-11, Colossians 1:15-20**). Figuratively, He meets us at Cana. He must be at our Cana, or all else is lost! On the way to our own Cana, we need to *THINK*! That's why this book is entitled, *Some **Thoughts** for the Journey to Cana: Christian Matrimony, Choice or Chance?*

As we journey to our Cana, we need to give deep *thought* to our decision to "become one" with another person. As you journey to Cana, it would be a good idea to have the Master come along to tell you a few things prior to your arrival. If He comes along for the journey, after dialoguing with Him, you may decide to turn back! If that's the case, consider it a blessing! If the three of you (i.e., you, your future spouse, and the Master) arrive at Cana at the same time, it's obviously His Will for you to go forward. If He has not gone on the journey with you, and heaven forbid, He is not in attendance, it's a good sign that it's not His Will, and that you are in for a horrible life!

No! The Master has instructed us that He is not *a* way, but the *only* way—*no one* can approach the Father *except* through Him (**John14: 6**).

In order to get the proverbial "ball" rolling, I've divided this book into six sections. They correspond to the six-week period that our Saint James Missionary Baptist Church Mid-Week Bible Study Group experienced as we explored the basic tenets of the Christian Faith as it related to Holy Matrimony. They are as follows:

- Marriage: Myth, Reality and the Bible

- Marriage: Religious Differences, To Yoke or Not to Yoke—That is the Question! Can Saved and Unsaved People Marry?

- Marriage: Finances—the Straw That Can Break Your Marital Back!

- Marriage: Family Background, "Excuse me—Point of Clarification Here—Am I Marrying *You* or Your *Mother?*"

- Marriage: Emotional and Physical Health. Do You Want a Spouse or a Patient?

- Marriage: Professional and Vocational Goals: "Hey, What D'bout Me?"

Our Framework

In the above areas, we will follow a basic framework, with some variation from chapter to chapter. The framework will reflect questions and observations about the particular area of concern (i.e., religious differences, financial concerns, etc.). The framework will allow you to find out, or at least get an indication, as to what both parties are bringing to the marital table.

This gives the participants an objective way to look at what's going on in their—as well as the other person's—"head," heart, soul, life, and mind.

The Framework Will Go As Follows:

I

First, we will look at an issue that experience has shown needs to be examined prior to getting married.

II

Second, we will look at the myths, or false and non-Biblical notions, surrounding this issue and marriage.

III

Third, we will look at the issue in light of the Holy Scriptures.

IV

Fourth, a series of danger signs—red flags if you will—will be outlined. These red flags should prompt you to begin asking questions of yourself as well as the other person.

V

Fifth, I will provide you with a set of questions you may want to ask yourself, as well as the person you are thinking about marrying. Following the questions, there is a section where you can write down questions that have since come to your mind that you feel need to be asked.

At this point, don't be afraid to ask questions. After all, if your engagement falls to pieces just because you asked a question, you really *didn't have much of a relationship in the first place*! Remember, if you don't ask now, the answers to those questions will come later, and you will curse the day you ever decided to give that person the time of day.

VI

Sixth, after you've raised a sufficient amount of questions, list ten reasons why you *should* marry that person. Following that, list ten reasons why you *should not* marry that person. Also, if *your* ego can stand it—why *should that person marry you*?

At this point, it will be necessary to bring in competent professional help. This means that you'll have to acquire the services of a trained and licensed professional to assist both of you as you weave through the issues that have been raised in your list of questions. If the issues cannot be resolved, what makes you think that slipping a ring on the other person's finger will change them—or *you* for that matter?

You may think that involving trained professionals at this point is an unnecessary intrusion into your relationship. However, the Bible counsels us that wise advice and counsel must be taken into consideration *prior* to making major decisions (**Proverbs 1:20-33, 14:15, 15:22**).

So as to facilitate this process, I've included reference material after each chapter to assist you in accessing professional assistance.

Hmmm, Maybe You Ought To Look At This Marriage Stuff A Little Closer!
THINK!

Thanks

As always, thanks goes to the great church, I serve as undershepherd, the Saint James Missionary Baptist Church of San Francisco's Bayview/Hunters Point area. Special kudos are in order for my friend and colleague of long standing, Rev. John Brinson. Rev. Brinson has given unselfishly of himself in many more ways than could be enumerated here. I want to thank my wife of nearly fifteen years, Patricia A. Williams for her support and encouragement as I've worked through this process.

Pastor Michael S. Williams, D.Min.
Saint James Missionary Baptist Church
San Francisco, California
Bayview /Hunters Point
Juneteenth 1999

CHAPTER 1

Marriage: Myth, Reality, And The Bible

I

Let's start at "square one." Lets examine the myths and fantasies that surround marriage in our society. Tragically, marriage, the Divinely ordained relationship between a man and woman, is entered into in many cases without a proper understanding of its essence and purpose. If that's the case, why do so many people—even Christians—make this terrible mistake? I think—and I stand to be corrected—it occurs because we've allowed the "World" to dictate to us what the purpose of marriage is. What do I mean? Look around you; it may be staring at you right now! It's the media! Media? Yes! What media?

- Television
- Movies
- Music

- Books and magazines

II

Myths, the Media, and Marriage

An old saying—but one nonetheless true—informs us that sex *sells*. The advertisement world knows that if it wants to push a particular product, just lace it with suggestive or explicit intimacy, etc., and sex! For the mass media, sex = love. But, hey, think about it, you can have *sex* with a person and *not love* that person! What makes you think physical contact = love? Two prizefighters can climb into a ring, and pound away at each other, but just because their bodies happen to collide that does not mean they love each other!

Television programs and movies can lead us to believe that all we have to do is to "hook-up" with that special "someone," and through intimacy, all of our troubles will be solved!

I marvel at how the daytime "Soaps" tell us relationships can be formed solely on the basis of what the scriptwriters deem to be "love" (which equals sex). "But Marsha, I *love* you!" "But Bill—I was *in love* with you last week, but this week I'm in *love* with George." BLAH, BLAH, BLAH! A close look at the "Soaps" will betray the fact that within the course of a year, Bill, Marsha, Tad, Brooke, etc., will all divorce each other, marry different characters on the show, and by the end of the year, divorce and marry each other all over again!

The movies are no better! They project the physically appealing aspects of our favorite movie "stars" in such a way as to make us want to experience the same emotions and activites that we see *projected* on the screen.

I deliberately use the word *projected* because that's all a movie or a TV show is—a **projection**! A movie or television program is merely a fantasy thrown on a wall in a darkened theater or sent into your home through your cable TV box in such a way as to grasp your attention.

The characters that have your attention on the movie or TV screen are **ACTORS**! Get it through your head, they are **ACTORS** and they are reading from a script! **It's not real**! They are human beings—just like you! They get paid to create a "realistic" setting that will grab your attention and make you pay attention to them! Get it through your head! They are **ACTORS**. They are wearing **MAKE-UP**! They are reciting **LINES FROM A SCRIPT**!

If they haven't made you
- Cry,
- Sexually stimulated,
- Scared,
- Happy,
- Sad,
- Angry,
- Want to "tune-in" again,

they have not done their job! So if what's happening on TV or the movie screen isn't real, why would you want to base an important decision like marriage upon how well an **ACTOR** recites his or her lines, or how well they wear their make-up? And just think about this—many of those "sexy hunks" and "sho' nuff *fiiiiine* wimins" that we drool over (no, that's not a typo, I said "wimins") in the movies and on TV that happen to fall "in love" and then proceed to fall "into the sack," actually hate each other. Some of them could be gay, and if that's the case, the only reason why they are even touching (and all the while mentally balancing their distaste for the opposite sex with their paycheck) their **ACTING** partner, is because they are getting paid to do so!

Remember Actors Are Merely Playing Parts! Do You Want To Build Your Life Upon An Image You've Seen On A Stage, Movie Screen, Or A TV Show?
THINK!

The same could be said about printed media: magazines, newspapers, books—especially so-called, "romance novels", etc. These "messengers" function as brainwashing tools the entertainment industry uses to convince us that unless *we* are *married*, or at least *intimately involved* with another person, then there must be something *wrong* with us.

The media sub-consciously brainwashes us by sending messages transmitted to our mind's memory bank that constantly tell us that if we *would* or *could* "just get married," or meet the "right person," then *everything* will be *all right*! My brother, my sister, if you have *not* met the Master yet, *anyone* you subsequently meet will be the wrong person!

Is It the Holy Spirit or is it Just an Urge?

There is a statement that members of my church can make that will send a chill down my spine. The statement is, "Pastor, the Spirit's telling me to...." Now before you accuse me of being a stuck-up Baptist that doesn't "believe in the movement of the Spirit," listen!

In over two and a half decades of ministry, I've just about seen it all when it comes to people being "led of the Spirit". I've seen:

- Persons get intimately involved with prison inmates, thinking they could "change" the inmate by surrendering themselves financially, professionally and sexually. The end result can be a broken heart, a beaten body, and/or a traumatized emotional state. The reason for pursuing the relationship was—"I was led of the Spirit."

- Persons commit adultery, wreak, and in turn ruin relationships—because they just knew that they were being "led of the Lord."

- Men that have no more business preaching than the proverbial "Man on the Moon" announcing that they have been "called to the ministry." In many cases, they have a bundle of emotional problems that can only cripple their walk with the Lord—as well as the church, which has the misfortune to "call" them to the pastorate!

- A "still small voice" (The Holy Spirit) tells you that you *should not* move from one job to another, but an *urge* you mistake for the Holy Spirit makes you do it because there is more money, perks, and prestige involved. As a result, you *feel* that you will be the "envy" of all of those people that told you that you would end up a failure. You get the job; it gets eliminated in a wave of downsizing, or you find out that jealous co-workers are backstabbing you. You then find out that your "dream job" *is* a dream—a nightmare, that is! But all the while—and up to that point—you felt "*led* of the Lord."

III

Go Ahead, Crack The Bible Open, Read It In Light Of Your Situation, I Dare You!

The above reasons—or should we say *excuses*—for entering into marriage are for the most part following *urges*—not the *Holy Spirit*! Let's look at several examples of following an urge instead of the Holy Spirit. At the end of this section, write some examples of your own, either from your own experience, or from the experiences of others.

Before we go further, let me run this by you:

Oh Come On! Who Are You Trying To Fool?

Look, the Bible is explicit! It does not condemn us for praying, dreaming or even wishing! It does however instruct us in the most unsympathetic terms that our emotional activity must be rooted in the Will of God!

- The Holy Spirit "edits" our prayers before they get to God—even if they were piously uttered in "Jesus' name" (**Romans 8:26-27**). Also, God will not honor a foolish request, even if you have fasted and prayed (**James 4:1-4**)!

- Our dreams *must* be rooted in *God's Will* (**Genesis 37, 41**).

- Idle daydreaming about what you'd "like my life to be like" about anything—*especially* marriage — is a waste of time (**Proverbs 12:11**)!

Time For a Reality Check!

As Christians, our *overall goal* is to *please* our Master. It's impossible to please Him if we substitute an *urge* for the Holy Spirit! Come on! How many times have you ever felt an urge to:
- Slap someone?
- Curse someone?
- "Go off" on someone?
- Go to your church's business meeting, quarterly conference, or charge conference and "lay someone's soul to rest" because "I just had to get it off of my chest"?

Think about it, *Christian*! *Acting* on an **urge** can get *you* into lots of trouble!

If it's not wise to marry someone for any of the silly non-Biblical excuses we discussed above—then what is the correct rationale for becoming "one" with another person? In order to "go there," we must compare "what I've always been taught" or "what I feel" with the Holy Scriptures! Just what does the Bible teach us about marriage? Keep on reading!

The Biblical Understanding of Marriage

As we move towards a Biblical understanding of marriage, understand this—the Bible describes situations that arise out of a male dominated culture. The society that produced the Bible was male dominated, or as scholars would say, **patriarchal (pay-tree-ark-al)**. This meant that the oldest male in the family was the "Head of the Household". This was true in both Old and New Testaments. The family was always known as the "Household of ____" (**Genesis 50:4, 1 Corinthians 16:15**).

The patriarch had certain duties. One duty was to make sure that his male guests lacked nothing relative to their comfort. Having a *male* guest in the house meant that literally all the "stops" were to be pulled out concerning his comfort and safety. If the guest was harmed or inconvenienced in any way, that meant the host was then disgraced. Disgrace, which meant exposure to hazards to the health and safety of the male guest, was to be avoided at all cost—even if it meant the *physical* and/or *sexual* abuse of the female members of the household (**Genesis 19:1-8**). Women were sometimes raped and murdered to preserve the *head of the household's honor* (**Judges 19:1-30**)!

The patriarch made all of the important decisions relative to the family members. The patriarch could choose his children's marital partner(s) (**Genesis 24:1-9, 28:1-2, 29:14-27, Exodus 2:21**). The patriarch chose the family's religion

(Joshua 24:15, Acts 16:1-34). The patriarch also had the power of life and death over the family **(Genesis 22:1-14, 34, 2 Samuel 13:20-36)**.

Another patriarchal aspect of the Bible, especially in Old Testament times, was a marital concept known as **polygamy (po-lig-gam-ee)**. This simply meant that the male was afforded the opportunity to have *several* wives **(Genesis 29, 2 Samuel 13:20-36, 1 Kings 11:1-4)**.

Another interesting aspect of Old Testament society was the fact that if a wife could not produce any children, especially male offspring, then the husband could have sex with his wife's female servant **(Genesis 16, 30:1-22)**, and hopefully, produce a male "in the wife's name." If no male heirs were produced, the household's leadership would fall to the eldest male within the household, which could be a slave! A male slave could carry on the family's male dominated leadership, but it was a distasteful option **(Genesis 15:1-4)**.

During New Testament times, it seems that **monogamy (mon-og-gam-ee)**, or marriage to only *one* person was the rule. However, the eldest male in the family was still the "head of the household" **(Matthew 1:18-19, Ephesians 5:21-31, Colossians 3:18-22, 1 Timothy 3:1-13, 1 Peter 3:1-7)**.

Obviously, the Bible describes the dynamics of male and female relationships for what was considered normal 2,500-4,000 years ago, but what about our time? I mean, rape and murder still occur, but those activities *are not* socially or legally acceptable for *our* time! Relationships containing more than one woman exist today. Just look at the daytime talk shows! You may even want to engage in such activity. If you do, it means that you will have to change your entire life around and do a lot of hiding, excuse making, and explaining.

Marriage for Our Time

There seems to be no record of an actual marriage ceremony within the Bible. However, the Bible speaks of marriage throughout both Old and New Testaments. And what it says about the marital arrangements has nothing to do with the media or our fantasies

First, and foremost, marriage between a man and a woman presupposes that God has done the selecting (**Genesis 2:20-25**). Second, whether we like it or not, when we marry someone, we become "one" with that person (**Genesis 2:24**). Now, that may sound real "holy," but Paul reminds us that being "one" with another person *may not* be the best thing for us (**1 Corinthians 6:16**). The key to enjoying Godly, sanctified, Christ centered "oneness," is to allow *God to be the matchmaker* (**Matthew 19:6**)!

If we allow God to choose our mate, it stands to reason we should be open to discerning if it's God's Perfect Will to marry in the first place. Hey! I know that someone reading this book is thinking, "But Rev, you don't understand, I'm lonely, and that's hell!" Look my brother, listen my sister, you don't know what *hell is* until you've gone outside of the Will of God and gotten married when our Lord *has not* prepared that special someone for you! I remember hearing a widower wisely say once, after he had been single for thirty years due to the death of his wife, that he would rather be *by himself*, than to be with the wrong person and *wish that he was by himself*!

God's Word gives us plenty of examples concerning how some Christians are actually called *to not marry*—period (**Matthew 19:1-12, 1 Corinthians 7:1-7**). If God has ordained a "single" life for you, marriage will hinder your walk with the Lord (**1 Corinthians 7:32-33**).

IV
Warning Signs!
Marriage: Examples of Mistaking an Urge for the Holy Spirit

- I am going to marry ___ because I feel sorry for him/her. After all, the Bible does say that the "strong must bear the burdens of the weak!"

- Physical contact (sexual arousal and activity) will solve *all* of my problems. (Mmmmy-my-my! Fornicating with ___ is great! If God made anything better than this, He must'ta kept it in Heaven for Himself!

- I feel an obligation towards ___. After all, s/he did help me take care of my father before he died! Plus s/he took care of me while I was out on disability. Even though I'm not all that crazy about the idea of marriage at this point in my life, and I really don't like ___, I think the Lord will bless me if I repay ___'s kindness towards me by (ick!) marrying him/her (Hmmm, I *hope* so!).

- I can "cure" ___'s sexual orientation, addictions and/or destructive patterns of behavior. I can pray that ___'s

_____ demon will leave him/her if we get married! For instance, although s/he has a demon within that humiliates me in public by hollering and screaming at me, it means I have just gotta fast and pray more! Jesus must have been speaking of me when He said, "Oh ye of little faith."

- _____ is a single parent. S/he needs my help in raising his/her children. _____'s no good "ex" left him/her with all of those babies! I'm going to be the parent that _____ needs for those kids! After all, didn't Jesus say, "Suffer the little children to come unto me"? Plus, since I'm unable to have kids, I'll just take on _____'s "ready made" situation—surely the Lord would want me to do this!!!

- _____'s professional life will enhance mine; his/her prestige will rub off on me. I can "prove" by my marrying_____ that God will bless you if you do what I'm doing! Gee, it will be *sooooooo* exciting to be married to a _____.

- S/he holds the position of _____ in the local church. Plus, s/he serves as _____ in our denomination! *Aggggggh*, I just gotta marry _____! It will fulfill my deepest needs; plus I will be the envy of all of those folks in my family and old neighborhood that claimed I'd never make anything out of myself! Wait till all of the naysayers see me hanging on _____'s arm when we stroll into the hotel at the next National meeting! I can just see their envious faces now! My, my, my! The Lord really does provide!! (And revenge is sweet—if I do say so myself!)

- S/he has a great singing voice; I love to hear ____ sing my favorite hymns! Surely, the Lord wants us together!

- ____ is unsaved, but I can lead ____ to Christ by marrying him/her.

- I need a spouse that's the only way I'll get that promotion! Surely the Lord wants me to advance and make more money!

- I will automatically stop being a homosexual if I marry ____. After all, I feel that the Lord would have me get "cured" this way! Gee, I hope no one finds out I'm gay (or bisexual, or feel like I should be the opposite sex); I'll even stop having sex with my "special friend." (Well at least, I'll *try* to!) I will get a spouse of the opposite sex; I'll "break" my "orientation" to ____ slowly (after we're married—or after s/he arrives home early and catches me with my—a-hem *friend!*). But one thing I will say; my future spouse's sibling (one that is the same sex as me) is *sooooooo* cute! Tell me the Lord doesn't provide! Hmmm, I can't wait to get to know him/her better! In fact, that's why I feel God put ____ and me together!

- All of my friends will envy me if I marry ____. I just *feel* as if this is the Lord's way of blessing me!

- ____ will be my "trophy." My friends will wonder, "How did ____ snag a man/woman that's so "____." See what happens when you tithe?

- We have similar professional backgrounds; therefore, the Lord must want us to be together!

- I feel that if I can just marry a ____, then my walk with Christ will be complete!

- I feel that the Lord wants me to marry ____. That way, I can help ____ with his/her professional duties.

- Since I have such a crummy relationship with my parents, I feel that the Lord has sent ____ into my life to be my mommy/daddy.

- Since I kinda "blew it" with *my* child, I feel that the Lord is calling me to be ____'s parent. Hmmm, I'll marry him/her and gain a spouse, a child, and a lover! Surely, the Lord would back me up on this one!

- I feel *led* to marry ____. That way, I can get out of my parent's house! Ain't it just somethin' how the Lord works?

Now, Come Up With Some Of Your Own! Don't Be Ashamed, No One Is Looking!

1. _____
2. _____
3. _____
4. _____

The Christian Model for Marriage

Now that we have looked at the myths and realities surrounding marriage along with the Biblical customs and teachings concerning marriage, I want to close this chapter by pointing you to the model that the Bible gives us for true Christian marriage.

Why am I taking time to do this? Because I want you to you to realize that there exist *no* legitimate models for Christian marriage amongst us human beings! I don't care if you had the world's greatest parents or grandparents! I don't care if a certain married couple happens to be your best friends, and you think that they are the role models to end all role models! I don't care if you were in your favorite couple's wedding and you began to cry because it was "just *sooooo* precious!" *Don't you dare model your marriage after them*! You *don't know* what they have to do to maintain a viable relationship—in other words, the late Flip Wilson was incorrect when he stated, "What you see is what you get." You *do not know* what it *costs* to keep their *business behind closed doors*! If *God* doesn't judge a book by its cover (**1**

Samuel 16:7)—and that's a mighty big *if*—why should you? Besides, you may have cried at their wedding because you thought it was *sooooooo* precious, but they may be crying now in hopelessness, wishing that they had never met each other!

The *only* legitimate model for a Christian marriage is that which reflects the relationship between God and His people (**Exodus 20:1-4, Hosea 1, Isaiah 54:1-6**), and Christ and His Church (**Ephesians 5:21-32, Revelation 21: 2-9, 22:17**).

If you confessed Jesus Christ to be your Savior and Lord, and then you will literally seek, through the power of the Holy Spirit, to obey His Will. You will be obedient, if you *are not*, you won't. But if you *are* God's child and *choose* to be disobedient, prepare to get locked into a marital situation that may *traumatize* your life in ways you never dreamed of!

If your planned marriage reflects the Biblical model, then you are on the road to success; if not, buckle up because you are in for a bumpy ride! Hold on, because you have bought a *one-way* ticket to marital hell!

Having said all of this, let's begin the next chapter by looking at some issues you should think about on your journey to Cana.

CHAPTER 2

Marriage: Religious Differences, To Yoke or Not to Yoke—That is The Question! Can Saved and Unsaved People Marry?

I

There's a fundamental issue you *must* consider on the way to Cana: Is my intended spouse saved or *not*? In two contexts, Paul explicitly teaches us that: a) who ever we become intimate with—we become "one" with (**1 Corinthians 6:16**); he also says that b) it's dangerous to be "yoked" with an unbeliever (**2 Corinthians 6:14-18**).

In agricultural settings, if the farmer uses a team of horses or oxen to pull a plow or wagon, then it would be wise for **both** the animals to at *least* be controllable and amenable to the authority of the one with the reins in his hands. If they are pulling in opposite directions, two things will happen. First, the wagon will tip over, thereby "spooking" one of the animals and possibly causing a runaway situation. Second, both animals may end up hurting themselves, the driver, and/or wasting the load.

Prior To Placing A Yoke Upon Your Neck by Saying, "I Do," You Had Better Make Sure That The Two Of You Are "Equally Yoked." After All, "The Two Shall Become One." Are You Sure You Want To Become "One" With _____?

In our case, as Christians, marriage demands that we be *equally yoked with a fellow believer*. If we are unequally yoked with an unbeliever, we will do more than tip our wagon over; we'll tip our life over! Our driver, Jesus, won't be injured, but our walk with Him can become compromised and difficult.

If you don't remember anything from this chapter, keep this in mind: you will *never* rise any higher than the people you associate with will(**Psalms 1, Proverbs 1:10-19, Hebrews 10:23-25**).

Having said that, a Christian should *never* even consider dating a non-believer—let alone marrying one. To do so will turn your dreams into nightmares. Now, let's look at the **PROBLEM** of being **UNEQUALLY YOKED**.

II

Warning!
Bowing To Social Pressure Instead Of Christ Can Destroy Us! Social Pressure Comes In Many Forms
Bowing To Social Pressure Can Have Us Unequally Yoked

Here are some *Satanically* inspired social pressures that can rush you to the *Devil's* altar:

- You had better get married soon; you are not getting any younger!

- I've got to marry ____. After all s/he is older than I am. That automatically makes ____ mature!

- I've got to marry ____. S/he is younger than I am; I like dating and socializing with younger ____. I get to be their parent. I have a crummy relationship with my kids. I will marry ____. I will get a child and a lover! What a winning hand! I can then "mold" ____'s character! Since men/women my age have too many hang ups, this way, I'll treat ____'s life like a chalk board and write what ever I want to on it—surely God wants this to happen!

- Get married to the next available person because there is a shortage of eligible singles! Get an unsaved one if necessary! Surely, God wouldn't want you to be lonely, would He?

- You need a spouse to advance professionally even though ____ is not saved; at least s/he is an *ok* person.

- Who are you to judge as to whether ____ should be saved or not? After all, who says that we have to worship God the same way?

- Hey! Who am I going to listen to, that *stupid preacher* or my *feelings*? Besides what does he know? ____ sexually stimulates me, and the fornication is literally *screaming*! What better way to have my cake and eat it too? I can have my sexual needs legitimated by marriage—plus I can evangelize ____ at the same time! Besides, didn't Jesus tell us to go everywhere? Surely, the Lord wouldn't have a problem with that—would He now? Besides, I'm grown anyway!

II

Whoa! Time for a Reality Check! Look for Some, All, or Other Signs That You Are Headed for Danger!

Put the brakes on and begin to **THINK!**

- Marrying an unsaved person *will* draw you away from God. This will in turn cause you to act out of character (**1 Kings 11:1-8, 16: 29-32, 18:4-19, 21:1-15**).

- An unsaved person *will* ridicule your faith when life takes a turn for the worse (**Job 2:9-10, Psalms 22:7-8**).

- That *person's* spirit will become *one* with *yours* (**1 Corinthians 6:12-20**). According to the Bible, getting involved with ungodly people has overwhelmed persons stronger than you (**Judges 16, Matthew 14: 1-12**)!

- That unsaved person will, by their intimate presence in your life, turn your heart away from the Lord (**1 Kings 11:1-8**). You will end up doing things that were unthinkable prior to your involvement with that person. Solomon did—what makes *you* think *you're* so special?

IV

Look Out for the Danger Signals

Hey! Start giving this thing a close look! There are danger signs popping up all around you; take the rose colored glasses off—you'll see them!

- S/he only goes to church with you if you ask, beg, threaten, or plead—and then unwillingly. While there, it's obvious s/he doesn't want to be there, because s/he fidgets all through the service.

- ____ claims that Sunday is his/her day to "cool out" and "sleep in."

- S/he entices you to live a compromised life; after all, you do have to prove that you love them, don't you? Plus who are you to judge someone else?

- They imply that your devotion to the Lord makes you a religious fanatic; this always leads to a mockery of God.

- They refuse to go to church with you, but invite you to the Kingdom Hall, Mormon Temple, mosque or ashram with them to hear their guru.

- ____ belongs to a religious group that is hostile to Christ and the Church.

- They belong to a group that does not worship in a Biblical manner. When you question it, they respond, "Hey, what's the difference, we're all worshiping the same *god* aren't we?" If you can answer "yes" to that question, then marriage is *not* what you need; it's Bible study!

- ____ claims that s/he has studied all of the major religions and found them to be basically the same, after all "Jesus has *some* good points, but so does Buddha, and Mohammed."

V
Now, Start Thinking!
Before You Holler "Giddy-Yup," I Want To Warn You About Two Other Types of Individuals You Should Not Consider Marrying Or Dating!

All Christians should be *obedient*. If you have confessed Jesus to be your Lord and Savior, you will, through the power of the Holy Spirit, seek to literally walk lock step with Him. In other words, you will seek to please Him. The only way to *please* Him is to *obey* Him. As Dietrich Bonhoeffer, the great Lutheran pastor/theologian executed by the Nazis prior to the end of World War II, said, *"Only* he who *believes* is *obedient,* and only he who is *obedient believes."*[1]

---

[1] Dietrich Bonhoeffer, *The Cost of Discipleship* (New York: Simon & Schuster Press, 1995), 63.

If you are obedient, then there are two types of persons you should *never* under *any* circumstances consider marrying. First, if you are a Christian and you are dating a fellow Christian, you need to be aware that just because the two of you are believers, it *may not* be God's Will for the two of you to marry!

What makes you think that just because you are both believers that God wants the two of you together? If the two of you are all *that* saved, then the both of you are on the same wavelength. This means that the signal you receive will not automatically say, "Go ahead and let's get married." Both of your "signals" will tell you to "wait on the Lord and to seek out His Will," even if it *goes against* everything we (think) we want (**Psalms 27:14, Isaiah 40:27-31, 55:8-9, Matthew 26: 36-39**). So, you see, when it comes to "weeding out" potential mates, remember—just because a person is saved, *it doesn't mean* that God wants the two of you together! Marrying a believer—and that is the only type of person you should consider marrying—could be a disaster if it's not God's Will for the two of you to "become one." And remember, maybe the Lord doesn't want the two of you to become "one." Maybe the Lord has another believer "out there" that He wants you to become "one" with!

Second, remember, an unsaved person can attend church also. That person can even hold a high office! But stop and think! Unsaved persons should be automatically deleted from your social life; we've established that. However the Christian that is *immature* in the Faith (**1 Corinthians 3: 1-4, 1 Timothy 5:21-22**) can be just as hazardous to your life as an *unbeliever*. In fact, an *immature* Christian is by definition, *carnal* (**1 Corinthians 3:1-4**), that is to say immature. In other words, they have a lot of growing to do before they are ready for a huge step like marriage! To marry a person like that will send your life into a tailspin that could take years—if ever—to exit!

Questions that Should Be Asked

First, of yourself:

1. What am I doing dating, or even contemplating, marrying an unsaved person?
2. ____ is saved, but is very "silly." S/he has no ambition or drive. S/he doesn't mind attending church with me, but it doesn't take much for us to get into an argument. ____ thinks that it's ok to miss Bible study—because it occurs on "hump day (Wednesday)." That's when ____ thinks we should spend some "quality time" with each other (translated *me*).
3. I have to literally beg ____ to come to church with me. All during the service, ____ squirms and fidgets. ____ also makes smart comments under his/her breath about "all of the hypocrites in church," and while the pastor was preaching, s/he kept mumbling—"I'm hungry, whenz' he gonna finish?"
4. ____ doesn't want me to go to Bible Study; s/he just wants to come over to my house and fornicate or watch videos. I must admit, s/he is an excellent sex partner—but why am I starting to come up with more excuses to be with ____ and miss church?
5. I know that what I'm doing is wrong—and s/he constantly belittles me concerning my faith—but besides

that, s/he's really a good person! Hey wait a minute—is my self esteem that low?

Come Up With Some Excuses of Your Own! Hey—No One Is Looking! This Will Be Our Little Secret!

6. _____
7. _____
8. _____
9. _____
10. _____

Work Time!

All right, write down ten reasons why you *should* marry or date an unsaved person.

1. _____
2. _____
3. _____
4. _____
5. _____
6. _____
7. _____
8. _____
9. _____
10. _____

Hmmm, if you came up with any positive reasons for marrying a person outside of the Will of the Lord, go back and prayerfully re-read this chapter!

Now write down at least ten reasons as to why you should *not* marry an unsaved person.

1. _____
2. _____
3. _____
4. _____
5. _____
6. _____
7. _____
8. _____
9. _____
10. _____

As you go through the reasons for dealing with a person that's unsaved, I would advise you to do two things. First, ask yourself why you are putting yourself at risk. Second, you need to make an appointment to seek advice from your pastor! Don't think of your pastor as someone to hide from; trust me, he'll know if there is something wrong with you. After all, the purpose of pastoral leadership is to protect you from dangers you don't see (**Ephesians 4:11, Hebrews 13:17**).

Remember the operative word for this book is:

THINK!

It won't kill you—it may even do you some good!

CHAPTER 3

I
Marriage: Money—The Straw That Can Break Your Marital Back!

You may not want to believe it, but unrealized or unresolved conflicts over money will rip your marriage to shreds quicker than adultery! In all too many cases, potentially good Christian marriages are ruined, strained, or ended because the couple did not know what each other's view of money was, and how "oneness" can lead to a financial reign of terror.

There is only one way to handle money—the right way. Any other way will set in motion a destructive cycle of money problems that will take years to resolve—if ever! After all, God may choose to *not* bail you out of the financial pickle that you've gotten yourself into. God's love can be hotter than any Sun in outer space and more devastating than any volcano **(Proverbs 3:11-12, Hebrews 12: 5-13)**.

Why? Because He may want to teach you to listen to Him in the first place and not just leap into a marital situation just because you "feel that it's time." A reckless decision to marry someone and not reflect on how both of your views concerning money square with the Word of God can cause financial ruin, emotional strain, and sadly enough, physical violence and even murder.

The topic of money is very *touchy*. This is as it should be! To ask about a person's financial status for no other reason than being nosy can touch off quite an explosion! However, engaged couples must be extremely candid about their understanding of money and its place in their lives. Better to find out **NOW**, than to wait till **AFTER THE WEDDING** and find that you have literally participated in your financial destruction by marrying someone whose views about money are contrary to yours! Internationally known Christian financial advisor, Larry Burkett says:

> By being candid about your attitudes and methods of money management, you can discover some of the following core values and attitudes that the two of you have.

- Selfishness versus cooperation
- Pride versus humility
- Self-control versus impulsiveness
- Greed versus generosity
- Sacrifice versus immediate self-gratification
- Your patterns of decision making
- Priority of eternal versus earthly values
- Planning versus being disorganized[1]

---

[1] Larry Burkett with Michael E. Taylor *Money Before Marriage: A Financial Workbook for Engaged Couples* (Chicago: Moody Press, 1996), 16-17.

If You Marry A Financially Irresponsible Person, Their Debts, Spending Habits, And Credit Record May...

...Merge With Yours In A Very Unpleasant Way! Prior To Reaching Cana, You Need To Study Each Other's Spending Patterns And Debt Profile! You Wouldn't Want To Find Out Too Late That S/He's A DeadBeat! A Financially Irresponsible Person Will Destroy In A Few Months What Took You Years To Build! Remember, "The Two Shall Become One!"

II

WARNING!
Myths, Money, and Marriage: Possible Warning Signs

Remember, **THINK!**

- S/he has never had to think of anyone but him/herself, but when we get married, this will all change!

- I just write checks and don't bother to balance my checkbook; s/he doesn't do this, but s/he will have to accept me as I am!

- For me, bankruptcy is a financial planning tool. I don't worry about my credit rating, so why should ____?

- What I make is *my money*!

- The amount of money I make is my business, not ____'s. When we get married, I don't see why I'd have to tell him/her even then!

- I think that when creditors call my job demanding payment, it's ok to have my co-worker tell them I'm not here today. After all—that's what friendship is all about! Plus, we're Christians and we are *supposed* to help each other!

- It's ok to owe everyone at church and at work.

- Wow, s/he has a lot of credit cards; I just can't wait to marry him/her. I screwed up my credit. So, s/he will have to give me credit cards also, after all the "two shall become one."

- I can't make my car notes on time; I'm in the process of hiding my car in my friend's garage. Who do those greedy finance people think they are? I'll pay them when I get ready!

- When a creditor calls, your future spouse screams at them, "If you are so smart, why did you lend the money to me in the first place?"

- Who needs to plan for the future? Besides, I've never owned anything—plus, I'm gonna die anyway!

- Purchasing insurance is a scheme to get money out of folks! Plus, if we buy an insurance policy, I'll die and ____ will marry ____ and they'll have a good time with the proceeds from *my* policy! *Wellllllllllllllllllll*, it may happen, but it will be over my dead body!

- Whenever you suggest that the two of you speak of planning for your financial future s/he screams "Get thee behind me, Satan!"

- All of my money goes to support my ____. My ____ doesn't want me to marry you, because s/he thinks that in doing so, the "gravy train" will screech to a halt.
- ____ doesn't work on a regular basis. S/he claims that to hold a regular job means that you have "sold out to the establishment."

- Your future spouse calls you at work demanding that you loan them money, "Cause I have a *bill* to pay." But s/he never tells you what type of bill it is!

- Your future spouse sits in his/her filth every day and scorns you for working. But that person always "bums" money from you.

- Money seems to "burn a hole" in ____'s pocket.

- Your future spouse's attitude is: "Why save—spend it now!"

- Your future spouse is secretive about his/her benefits package. S/he also refuses to remove his/her ____ from the benefits and place you as beneficiary, because, "Look—you will be my spouse—but ____ will always be my ____."

Time for a Reality Check

If you want to have a successful marriage, one thing you must **THINK** about prior to your arrival at Cana is—just how will we handle our finances? Give some thought to the following:

- "The two shall become one" means that the two credit histories will merge—and perhaps in a very unpleasant way.

- It's important for prospective spouses to have a full understanding of how the other party handles money.

- If you prospective spouse handles money in a way that's contrary to your method, and it makes you feel uncomfortable—what makes you think that person will change just because you put a ring on his/her finger?

- An irresponsible attitude towards money could have a devastating effect upon key factors in your life. Your professional performance will suffer, you won't be able to think coherently, and you will literally drown in debt. It's at that point you will begin to view options that can perhaps exacerbate the problem, i.e., gambling (not because you are addicted—not *you*!) to see if the Lord may work through the slot machine or the Lotto ticket. Drug abuse, extra-marital affairs, shopping, gossiping, stealing, or eating binges, as means of escape, are seen as viable options now that you've screwed up your life by marrying ____; why not dull it with some pain killers?

Biblical Reflections on the Proper Usage of Money

- First, realize that everything belongs to God (**Psalms 24**). He expects us to be good stewards over what He has *loaned* us.
- He will provide for all of our *needs* (**Psalms 23:1, Matthew 6:11, 24-34**).
- The Lord may not bail us out of foolish situations we've gotten ourselves into. He may just let us suffer for the long or short term so that we will learn from our mistakes (**2 Samuel 12:13-15**).
- Long range *financial planning* is *not* an *OBSCENE PHRASE* (**Proverbs 6:6-11, 7: 17-21, 10:4-5, 30:25-28**). In fact, the Bible teaches in no uncertain terms that everything must be "done decently and in order" (**1 Corinthians 14:40**). There is no Heavenly glory in living in a financially dysfunctional marriage!
- A person that refuses to take care of his/her family (i.e., spouse) is worse than an unbeliever (**1Timothy 5:8**)!
- A person that has the potential to bring financial ruin upon your head should be avoided like "the plague" (**Proverbs 11:29**).

THINK on These Things!

- *It's dangerous to co-sign for loans,* **Proverbs 11:15, 17:18, 20:16, and 22: 26-27, 27:13.**

- *The problem of laziness,* **Proverbs 6:6-11, 12:24, 27, 13:4, 14:23, 17:2, 19:24, 20:13, 21:25, 22:13, 24:30-34, 26,13-16, 29:19, 30:15-16**.

- *The key to handling debt,* **Proverbs 18:23. 21:20.**

- What *dead beats* are, **Psalms 37:21.**

- *The Christian response to moochers,* 2 Thessalonians 3:6-12.

IV

Danger Signs to Look For

Check it out! Are you or your future spouse financial disasters waiting to happen? The following warning flags could apply to either one of you or both.

- Because of a bad checking account record, a checking account can't be opened.

- S/he makes "good money" but never seems to have enough. This bears looking into (**John 12:1-6, 13:21-30**). What's the reason—hmmm?

- S/he has an "eat, drink, and be merry—for tomorrow we shall die" attitude (**1 Corinthians 15: 32**).

- It's obvious that a relative or friend is draining you or your future spouse of money. That means some one is either addicted to the "drainer" or happens to be the "drainers" co-dependent.

- Whenever the words or phrases—"save, cut back, sacrifice, put off till a more convenient time, plan," etc., are used concerning money, you are met with, "I denounce you, Satan—and all of your works!"

V

Work Time: A Suggested Process

Each party should disclose their current financial status to the other. This means everything! All financial documents, debts, credit reports, wage garnishments, back taxes, etc. must literally be "put out on the table."

The following questions may seem a bit nosy, or intrusive. But realize if any of these questions are relevant to either of your financial situations, it *will* become the other's problem! After all, "the two shall become one!" And as I've said before, that may not be a pleasant experience. Ask questions like:

Oh Come on, Don't Be Chicken!

1. Why do you spend more than you take in?

2. Why is that you live with your parents, you pay no rent or utilities—and yet you still have to BUM money from everyone?

3. Why did you have to file bankruptcy?

4. Why don't you have any insurance?

5. Why do you borrow all the time? You make more money than I do!

6. Who are those shady people that seem to make you nervous? Why do you talk in hushed tones around them? Why did you go into the other room and take a call from them and scream—"Look you gotta be patient, I'll get you the money as soon as possible"?—*YES*, I know what happens to people that don't pay the money they owe!

7. Do you have any lawsuits pending against you?

8. Are you current with your child support and/or alimony? If not, *why* not?

9. _____

10. _____

VI

Now it's Time To Get Some Helllllllllllllp!!!!

After potential problem areas are uncovered, it's time to bring in a qualified team of professionals. Marriage *will not* solve these problems; it will *only make them worse*! A person that doesn't want to improve and correct his/her destructive behavior may not be the person for you! At this point, seek the service of a **Certified Financial Planner**, and if necessary—a **tax attorney**, and a **Certified Public Accountant**. Remember, the "two shall become one." That means you will share tax liens, maxed out credit cards, bills, etc. Habits and attitudes concerning money will affect everyone involved; it can also affect your credit rating and job performance!

Remember!

- Your power and light company couldn't care less that you thought that it was joking—and didn't pay your bill because you wanted to "treat" yourself to a _____!

- Landlords can and will evict you if you don't pay your rent.

- Your finance company will boot you out of your house if you don't pay your mortgage.

- You will always be at the mercy of others if your debts constantly exceed your income.

- You can destroy in a few minutes what may have taken someone years to build.

- The District Attorney takes a dim view of the fact that you write checks, with nothing in the bank. S/he doesn't care whether your "mommy" or "daddy" never told you how to balance a checkbook, and you keep writing checks!

- You will bounce from job to job and never advance if you were never taught such basic skills as—showing up on time, doing the work assigned, not going AWOL "cause I needed a break," and that you feel that to work means that you have "sold out to the establishment."

Ten Reasons for Marrying a Financially Immature Person

1. _____
2. _____
3. _____
4. _____
5. _____
6. _____
7. _____
8. _____
9. _____
10. _____

Ten Reasons for Not Marrying a Financially Immature Person

1. _____
2. _____
3. _____
4. _____
5. _____
6. _____
7. _____
8. _____
9. _____
10. _____

Resources for Handling Money Issues

1) For **legal issues** arising from financial issues, I recommend that you consult your local bar association. Many bar associations have low fee referral service. In most cases, for a nominal fee, you can have a private consultation with an attorney that specializes in your area of concern. For information concerning your local bar association's legal referral service, contact:

BOOKS

Larry Burkett and Michael E. Taylor *Money Before Marriage: A Financial Workbook for Engaged Couples*. Chicago: Moody Press, 1996.

Attorney Robin Leonard, *Nolo's Law Form Kit Rebuild Your Credit*. Berkeley, CA: Nolo Press, 1994

Pastor Willie Richardson *Reclaiming the Urban Family: How to Mobilize the Church as a Family Training Center.* Grand Rapids, MI: ZondervanPublishingHouse, 1996.

NOTE: Pastor Richardson's chapter on Christian Stewardship (pages 141-156) gives an excellent summary of the problems of and solutions to poor money management skills. Don't you dare *think* about going to Cana without reading it! All of the above resources can save you a lot grief!

CHAPTER 4

Marriage and Family Relationships: "Excuse Me—Point Of Clarification Here, Am I Marrying You or Your Mother?"

I

Make no mistake, the manner in which we were raised, as well as the people that reared us, played a crucial role in how we behave as adults. A person's environment has a tendency to "rub off" on them! For better or for worst, remember, the "two shall become one."

II

WARNING!
Myths, Family Background, And Marriage (Signs Of Possible Trouble) If The Following Examples Apply To Either You Or Your Future Spouse—Apply The Emergency Brake!

- I've never had to think about anyone but myself; when we get married, by magic, I'll change.

- When I go over to ____'s parent's house for the holidays, ____ totally ignores me; the family refers to me as "you."

- I went to ____'s mother's birthday party, and all of ____'s ____ subjected me to an interrogation. They then dismissed me, shut the door and discussed me. They then took a vote as to whether I was "worthy" to marry their ____. ____ told me, "That's just the way it's in my family, and *you'll have to learn to accept it.*" From what I understand, the vote was close. Right now, ____ is sweating because s/he always does what his/her family tells him/her to do!

- ____'s 8-year-old nephew kicked me in the shins and told me he didn't want me to be his uncle/aunt.

- ____'s teenaged son/daughter got in my face and informed me that his/her ____ told him/her, "my ____ told me, since you ain't my real ____, I don't have to do what you say!"

- My future in-laws constantly tell me how wonderful my future spouse's late or ex-spouse was/is *really* special. S/he was a "real" husband/wife!

- My future spouse's crippled and elderly parents wait on him/her "hand and foot." They have to do this because even though s/he is grown, s/he is "just a child, and needs his/her rest" (*46 years old*—gimme a break!?). They also inform you that those narrow-minded supervisors at his/her last (6 jobs in the last 2 months) are out to get him/her, that's why s/he doesn't work. "In fact," they say, "even though we're on a fixed income and we're barely making it, we are going to take a second mortgage out on our home in order to hire a lawyer so 'our widdle baby' can sue his last employer! We'll just draw the equity down in our home and give ____ the money. That will make sure that s/he can hire an attorney as well as get into the 'rehab' program s/he says is *sooooooooo* wonderful."

- Your relatives tell you that even though *you're* marrying ____, "*we're* still *your* family." Your future in-laws ask you, "Why are you taking ____ from us? That's okay we're *still* ____'s family!"

- ____'s family has a tradition of being violent, exploitative and abusive. All the men beat their wives/girlfriends. The women hide money from their husbands. The grandchildren physically and financially abuse their elders.

- Having a lot of "traffic" is considered normal, even at odd hours of the day and night.

- ____ is grown, chronologically, but is very immature. ____ thinks that the 24 hour notice from the phone company is either a joke, or says "Well, when ya gonna pay it?" When you insist that it must be paid, s/he screams, "Get thee behind me, Satan! I denounce you and all of your works! Besides, you're selfish anyway!" What'a 'bout me? What'a 'bout me? What'a 'bout *meeeeeeeeeeeeeeeeeeeeeeeee?*

- ____ is grown, has a good job, is an otherwise responsible person—but has never lived away from home. The thought of that person leaving home is causing ____'s relatives to go into "withdrawal." All of a sudden as s/he begins to rethink the decision to leave home, his/her family starts to go back to normal (?).

III

The Bible Speaks to Keeping the Proper Perspective Relative to A Person's Family Background.

- First, we have to ask the question: Who's getting married—you and ____, or you and ____'s relatives, or vice versa? The Bible tells us that the *spouses shall become one flesh*, not the *spouse + their children*, or the *spouse + their parents*, or the *spouse + their "ex"* (**Genesis 2:24-25**).

- Second, we have to also realize that Jesus limits members of His family to "those that do the will of my Father in Heaven" (**Matthew 12:46-50**). This concept is radically different from what the world considers "family." Plus—and this may come as a shock to all of you co-dependents out there—following Jesus will cause problems with your family (**Matthew 10:34-37**).

- Paul pushes Jesus' point even further by informing us that Christians are members of God's Family, not through Abraham, *not by birth*, but by our *relationship with Jesus Christ* (**Romans 4-5, 9-11, Galatians 3:15-18, Ephesians 2:11-22**). He also reminds us that we are Jesus' Body (**1 Corinthians 12**)!

- Third, unlike your unsaved friends and relatives, you have been born *twice*; they have only been born *once* (**John 3**). You have been born into God's Family; therefore, you may address Him as *Father* (**Romans 8:12-17, Galatians 4: 1-7**)! The unsaved can *only* know Him as *Creator*. The Christian knows God as *Creator and Father* because of the Son of God (**Romans 8:15 and Galatians 4:1-7**).

- Fourth, being a Christian *will* cause friction with *unsaved* relatives (**Mark 13: 9-13**).

IV

Yoo-Hoo! Time for a Reality Check!

- A person, due to family dynamics or obligations, may not be ready or have the time for a marriage because raising children or taking care of sick relatives leaves them *no time* for marriage.

- Don't expect to automatically become "mommy" or "daddy" to their children just because you've slipped a ring on their parent's finger.

- Expect *possible* problems from your future spouse's "ex" (spouse, boyfriend/girlfriend), especially if they have children in common.

- Expect possible problems from ____'s "ex," even if there are *no* children involved. Why? Because maybe the "ex" killed their relationship with ____ due to their childish behavior. Now they are angry and will use every silly spiteful thing they can think of to tear your relationship up.

V

It's Question Time Again!!! Don't Be Afraid To Ask:

a) Why do you disappear off the face of the earth every ___ and your mother tells me it's none of my business where you are?

b) Why is it ok for little ____ to kick me, spit on me, and inform me that _____ (your "ex," your "ex" in-laws, your relatives) says I better not put my blank-ed-d-blank hands on them?

c) Why is it when I mention that it bothers me that you need to borrow money from me because your (grown) child can't manage his/her money, you scream, "Just shut-up and gimme the money—I know ____ has a few problems, but dat's my *chiiiiiiiiiiiiiiiiiiiiiiiiiiiiiild*!" (____ is technically grown, but at 24 years old, s/he's "just a baby?") "S/he's my *chhhhhhhhhhhhiiiiiiiiiiiiidddddddddd*! Gimme the $500.00! I need it; s/he's my *chhhhhhhhild*!!!! I don't care if the phone gets cut off! Gimme 'da money, s/he's my child!"

d) Like everyone in your family, whenever you get angry, you rip something up; does that extend to other *people* too (*like me*)?

e) How do you feel about pre-marital counseling?

f) Why do you think that counseling is the "work of the devil?"

g) Why do you think that counseling is letting "outsiders get in your business?"

h) Outside of paying child support, why, all of a sudden, have you taken a big interest in your "ex?" Why, all of a sudden, is s/he so great?

Now—Come up with some of your own!!
Remember—THINK!

i) _____
j) _____
k) _____
l) _____

VI

Suggested Process

It's thinking time!

- Both parties should consider taking some time to put "everything on the table" concerning their family obligations. Then, in light of the Bible, they should carefully examine *if they have the time* for marrying someone at this particular time in their life

- Both parties should be honest about problems that they have with the other's current family situation and how it could affect the marriage. Be honest *now*, because it will come up *later*—possibly with violent consequences

After potential problem areas are uncovered, it's time to seek out professional help so as to unravel potentially dangerous problems in your relationship. Professional help can also assist you in uncovering the true motives for your desire to marry. Don't be afraid! A trained therapist can help *you* sort through the reasons as to why you think that this relationship is for *you*! God can speak through that person if you are willing to listen (**Numbers 22: 22-35**)! Remember, "the two shall become one!"

- If clear boundaries are not maintained, whatever sickness they may have in their family system will affect you!

- Remnants of their previous relationships will crop up and throw your life off balance

WORK TIME!
10 reasons *for* marrying a person with "unfinished business" relative to his/her family

1. _____
2. _____
3. _____
4. _____
5. _____
6. _____
7. _____
8. _____
9. _____
10. _____

10 Reasons for *not* marrying person with "unfinished business" relative to his/her family

1. _____
2. _____
3. _____
4. _____
5. _____
6. _____
7. _____
8. _____
9. _____
10. _____

Professional Resources for Family Background Issues

As far as assistance in sorting out marital and family issues, consult your local medical society if necessary. Also, check your Health Maintenance Organization's resource book. Most HMOs have a mental health component. Don't be afraid to "tell the therapist your business"; a trained professional can and will give you an objective reading of your situation. It will also be done in the strictest confidence! Either you let the therapist into your private "business," or it will fester and publicly explode—then *everyone* will be in your "business!"

CHAPTER 5

Marriage: Emotional and Physical Health: Do you Want a Spouse or a "Patient"?

I

Prior to setting a wedding date, ordering invitations, contracting with a caterer, arguing over who will sit where, and tangling with your "ex" as to whether your child from your previous relationship can be in the wedding, etc., you and your proposed spouse *must* sit down and make an assessment of each other's emotional and physical health. Any and *every* thing relative to a person's emotional and physical health *must* be put on the table.

Of course we promise to love each other "in sickness and in health," but if a person has a chronic physical or emotional problem, are you sure you can handle it? Is marriage this best thing for the two of you right now? Dating is one thing, but constantly catering to another person's illness is quite another! Remember—**THINK**!

If The Two Of You Were Actors, Would You Both Be Performing In The Same Play And On (Or At) The Same Stage?

Depending upon where a person "is" in life *must* be taken into consideration. In other words, what *stage* of life is s/he in? Our life stages have a lot to do with our emotional and physical health. For example, you need to ask the question, "What do I have in common with a person that happens to be middle aged and I'm a teenager? S/he is beginning to slow down, and I'm just getting started! S/he can't last as long as I can when we're on the basketball court."

A popular phrase of the late 1980s and early 1990s was: "Are we on the same page?" This was meant as a slang-like way of asking, "Are we going in the same direction?" If there is the possibility of marriage in your future, to ask if "we're on the same page" should mean, "Are we in the same, or at least similar stage of our life's journey?" If the two of you are Christians, then at least you are in the same "book." But even Christians, of different ages and experiences, will be undoubtedly on "different pages!"

Perhaps Gail Sheedy made one of the best articulations of life's "stages" in her book, *Passages: Predictable Crises of Adult Life*. For Sheedy, life is a clearly defined set of predictable stages. Unlike *exterior* changes such as weight, hair loss, or visible signs of aging, these life-altering changes occur *within* us. She refers to each stage as a "passage." According to Sheedy:

> During each of these passages, how we feel about our way of living will undergo subtle changes in four areas of perception. One is the interior sense of self in relation to others. A second is the proportion of safeness to danger we feel in our lives. A third is our perception of time—do we have plenty of it, or are we beginning to feel that time is running out? Last there will be some shift at the gut level our sense of aliveness or stagnation. These are the hazy sensations that compose the background

tone of living and shape the decisions on which we take action.[1]

If Sheedy's suggestion is correct, then we could safely assume that blindly plunging into another person's life—especially when they are going through a critical stage on their life's journey or vice versa—through an ill-timed marriage, *can* and *will* be a disaster! Such a union can in turn be dubbed an untimely event, which can upset a person's life cycle. She goes on to say:

> [For example] when financial reverses prompt a young person to quit school and go to work, when marriage does not happen at a hoped-for time, when a child is born unusually early or late, when people can't simply can't seem to find themselves and their occupational achievement is delayed—these are what we might call untimely events. They upset the sequence and rhythm of the expected life cycle. People whose lives have been shaped by such *untimely events* grope for some handle to explain what they did not anticipate.[2]

In trying to explain why life did not work out as planned, should you intervene in a person's life at the wrong time; there could be a problem in terms of you taking the blame for "me not being where I should be at this stage of my life"! Now, do you want that? **THINK!**

---

[1] Gail Sheedy, *Passages: Predictable Crises of Adult Life* (New York: Bantam Books, 1977), 30.
[2] Ibid., 31

If You Are Not Careful, You Could End Up With A Patient, Not A Spouse! Can You Handle It? THINK and PRAY it Through! Remember, "Count Up The Cost" (Luke 14:28).

Not knowing or understanding such things as where a person "is" in life is a recipe for disaster! Such lack of understanding will cause a break down in communication. And after all, what is communication other than being able to understand what another is saying? For instance, if you are in a crucial stage of your professional development and you have invested a great deal of time and energy in your career, marrying someone who perceives that they are in the "sunset" of life can be dangerous! After all, you may need to put in 60-80 hours per week to "make it" in your chosen field.

If your proposed spouse is facing retirement or has become complacent, then your "drive" could be interpreted as being "selfish." If you go through with marrying someone like that, be prepared for having, "What about me!" thrown at you. This will disrupt your rhythm and send you into a tailspin. When you then "crash and burn," be ready for self-incrimination and regret over missed opportunities—you may even grow to hate your spouse! Then even worse, prepare yourself for, "I told you that you were selfish and should have paid more attention to *us* (translated—*me*)." Why put yourself through it?

THINK!

Are you a single parent, struggling alone against all odds? Are you the primary caregiver for an ill relative? Then, it may not be the best time for either you or the person you are dating to even think about marriage! If you attempt to "become one" with another person at this stage of your life, your emotional plate may become so overwhelmed that you will end up losing everything you hold dear—to say nothing of your mind!

By implication, if engaged couples are unclear concerning these dynamics, all marriage plans should be either put off indefinitely or even cancelled. Not knowing or understanding which "life stage" a person is in will undoubtedly spell disaster! It's a one-way ticket to marriage *HELL*.

No matter how much you (think you) "love" someone, that person's emotional and physical health problems may put such a strain on your relationship that you may wish that they'd "drop out of sight" or even drop dead (oh yes, even the strongest Christians can begin to have those kinds of fantasies—especially when the reality of their spouse's chronic mental or physical condition begins to set in)!

The stress and strain of dealing with a physical or mental illness you are not prepared for can cause you to "go off the deep end" and do violence to the other person, yourself, or both (ever heard of murder/suicide?). Stronger people than you have "lost it" under the strain of things they were not prepared for! Remember, "the two shall become one!"[3]

---

[3] One of these days you will realize that what a person *does* for a living can be at complete variance with what s/he *is*. A person can be rational one minute and completely "off" the next—this can go for people with high social and professional rank! "Ex-Stanford Official, a Murder Suspect: Student, 21, Stabbed to Death in Connecticut." *The Palo Alto Daily News* (Palo Alto, California) January 19 1999. If that's true about persons with high rank and prestige, what makes you think *you're* so different? **THINK!**

IV

(Hey—Are You Takin' Any of This In?)

Myths, Emotional/Physical Health, And Marriage (Possible Warning Signs Of Trouble)

- S/he has a _____ condition. I resent the fact that it's an all-consuming issue, but when we get married, I'll change. Plus, I'd feel guilty if I left ____. Who would be there to take care of his/her ____ condition?

- I'm a health care professional—I can handle it!

- I took care of ____'s mother before she died. S/he has the same hereditary problem; ____'s mother died a slow, agonizing death. Watching her die like that took an emotional toll on me and strained my relationship with ____. S/he's starting to show signs of the illness, but I can handle it! Plus I'd feel kind of guilty if I were to leave ____ now! After we marry, it will all change! Hmmm, the wedding is in June, s/he is getting sicker everyday, it's March—I don't think s/he will die, but I can just see it now—taking care of ____ like I took care of his/her mother—hmmm. ____'s mother's illness made her suffer for 18 years before she passed away. I remember ____'s doctor telling us that this condition can linger for up to 30 years! Something about all of this doesn't seem right.

- S/he has severe issues surrounding men/women. S/he swore that the next person to "hurt" him/her would have to pay "big time." I'm different; I can handle it! The others couldn't deal with it, but I can! Besides s/he must really love me, s/he could have stabbed me to death with that meat cleaver s/he threw at me, but it stuck in the wall! If s/he didn't love me, s/he would have stabbed me. Look! See! S/he didn't stab me; s/he just took the cleaver and stabbed the wall 60 times. With every stab, s/he repeated my name! S/he also hollered, *"die-die-die-die"* with each wall stab! After that was over, we hopped in the sack and fornicated like there was no tomorrow! When it comes to love, ya gotta learn to deal with a person's insecurities!

- I'm a medical professional; I can handle anything! (Although since I've been with ____, I find myself self-prescribing a lot of drugs for my nerves. Hmmmm, I'm not an addict; I just need this stuff to cope with ____. As I said, I'm not an addict; I went to medical school!

- I'm a substance abuse counselor; I know how to handle emotional problems. ____'s drug use is a "piece of cake"; I've treated hundreds of people like him/her before—just think! A spouse and a client all wrapped into one! Surely, the Lord has put us together!

- S/he is secretive about all of the pills s/he has to take. S/he won't tell me what the problem is.

- S/he is in a codependent relationship with his/her relatives. When we get married, that will all change because, I will do everything I know to change ____'s emotional patterns. All I need to do is to be a great lover, buy flowers, remember his/her birthday, and everything will be "hunky-dory". This will be a piece of cake!

- When s/he observes me speaking to a member of the opposite sex, s/he automatically thinks we are flirting. S/he rants, raves, and generally makes an idiot out of him/herself. When we get married, this will all change!

- I need to stick with _____ like glue 'cause all of those low down women/men want ____. Even if it means making a scene, I will make ____ wish s/he had never spoke to *my* man/woman! When will all of those low-down-dirty folks realize that ____ is *my* man/woman!

Reality, Emotional and Physical Health, and Marriage

- Prior to getting married, both parties should be frank about the state of their emotional and physical health and not allow rose-colored, "romantic" notions color their thinking!

- If you are at a particular point in your professional life/career, and your future spouse has a disabling condition, take the rose colored glasses off and ask yourself: Can you afford to handle that *and* your professional obligations?

- What "Stage" of life are you and your future spouse in? Different stages require different ways of relating to life.

Are You Oil While S/He's Water? Can Persons With Your Types of Temperaments Actually Spend The Rest Of Your Lives Together? Think!

Also, significant differences in temperament, health, emotional issues, and age can make for a volatile mix of issues that can side-track ambitions, dreams, aspirations, and in due course cause professional, financial or vocational problems that may take years—if ever to resolve

- You may want to think twice before jumping into a situation that you are becoming increasingly aware of as being "way over you head" just because "I gave my word" or "I feel sorry for _____."

Are Ya' Still With Me?

The Bible Speaks To The Issue Of Taking On Situations That May Be Too Big For Us To Handle

- Do you want to spend the rest of your life (which may not e very long if you marry ____) with a person that has a lot of nresolved anger (**1 Kings 2: 1-9**)?

  Do you want to "become one" with a person that's *always* right (**Proverbs 9:7**)?

- Can you handle a person that dismantles everything that you *try to build up*, or worst yet, *has* dismantled everything you *built up **before** getting entangled with that person* (**Proverbs 14:1**)?

- Can you handle a person's addictive or "quirky" behavior? Right now its "cute" and "makes ____ so special," but how about the long term? How long will it remain cute (**Proverbs 20:1, 23:29-35**)?

- What can you do with a person that drains you emotionally, financially and/or professionally, and doesn't want to get any help because, it's the "work of the devil" or "it's letting outsiders into our business" (**Proverbs 11:29, 14:1**)?

- How about nagging? Will that really make you a better person to put yourself through that type of **HELL** (**Proverbs 17:1**)?

Have You Ever Asked—What Kind of Person Is S/He, Or More Importantly, What Type of Person Am I? Am I A Physics Text—Is S/He A Comic Book? Remember, Physics Books and Comic Books are Both Books—But Ask Yourself—Will you find them Both on the Same Shelf?

Closely related to knowing what "page" you and your proposed spouse happen to be on, is just what *types* of books are we? I use the term *type* deliberately. For example, all screwdrivers are screwdrivers, but all screwdrivers do not have the same function. In other words, you wouldn't use a Phillips head screw with a flat head screwdriver! Why? Because even though both tools are screwdrivers, both are different *types* of screwdrivers! The four-cornered Phillips head screwdriver will not be very effective with screws that are cut in such a way as to accommodate the single flat groove of a flat head screw. Don't take my word for it! As an assignment, why don't you get both screwdrivers and the type of screws they are meant to accommodate and then mix match the tools and screws? Then try to twist the screws into a piece of wood! I guarantee that your task will be either difficult or impossible!

Let me put it bluntly; just because you and your intended spouse are both Christians, it *does not mean that you are compatible*! Maybe you like the way his/her clothes fit. Maybe the fact that s/he teaches Sunday School has you thinking that the two of you were meant for each other.

Maybe you fell "in love" with the fact that s/he is a church musician. But listen—those *types* of reasons are *superficial!* Why? Because they all ignore his/her *personality type*!

I hate to burst your bubble, but there is more to your proposed spouse's personality than their church activities or how their clothes fit! If the *Lord* isn't impressed with our outside appearance, why should *we* (**1 Samuel 16:17**)?

Suggested Process

Both parties should be open and up front about possible emotional or physical ailments they may have, or are prone to get. Some of these things can't be predicted, but ask yourself, would you want to marry someone that has a serious ailment, and they are hiding it from you? Or vice versa? What else will they hide from you? *How many surprises can you stand*? Don't be afraid to ask the other person—as well as yourself— just what are the both of us bringing to the marital table?

Time To Head To The Doctor's Office! Pronto!

Put The Pedal To The Metal!

Go to each other's doctors and emotional health professionals and be frank about each other's conditions. You

don't have to be honest and up front, but if you aren't, especially about something that could complicate another person's life, what does that say about you?
Don't be afraid to ask questions like:

a) Why is it when I ask why your nose runs constantly, you tell me not to worry, because it's a condition you picked up in "Nam" (But you were never in the service! Plus the war *ended* in 1975, and *you were born* in 1968!)?

b) Why do you have these fits of anger, and you articulate your rage by kicking what or who ever is near?

c) Why is it that you've wrecked your car several times because you pass out behind the wheel? When I asked you why, you told me its "none of my business" and that I will "just have to learn to live with it."

d) I have genital herpes. If I tell ____ about it, I wonder if s/he will leave me. Should I wait till after the wedding? Should I tell him/her now?

What Are The Two Of You Bringing To The Marital Table? Hmmm?

THINK!

Lets Step Back For A Minute, Let Me Run This By You Again

Remember, earlier we spoke of the different "personality types." A way to get an idea as to what type of personality you and you future spouse have is to, under the guidance of a qualified professional, take the Myers-Briggs Type Indicator ® test.[3]

After potential problem areas are uncovered, it's time to seek out professional help so as to identify potential problem areas that could dribble or destroy not just your relationship, but also either you or the other person. Professional help can assist you discern possible problem areas. The professionals that should be brought in are physicians and emotional health professionals. Remember, the "two shall become one."

---

[3] Says Renee Baron, "[Learning] about personality types can also help us make more conscious choices in relationships. It will enable us to see why, although we are initially drawn to a certain type of person, we are ready to tear our hair out about their habits and "shortcomings" a few months later. Sometimes the very qualities that attracted us to someone in the first place are the ones that we find ourselves trying to change later on." Renee Baron, *What Type of Person am I?: Discover Who You Really Are* (New York: Penguin-Putnam, Inc. 1998), 2. The Myers-Briggs Type Indicator ® presupposes that there are basically sixteen types of personalities. For an introduction to the various types, I recommend that you obtain Baron's book and carefully read Chapter 1, pages 1-6. In order to find out what your type is, carefully read Chapter 7, pages 44-47. But as I mentioned earlier, in order to get the most out of this process, a qualified professional must administer the test.

THINK ABOUT THIS!

- If you want to care for a person with a chronic illness, and you are fully aware of the implications, prepare yourself for a major and permanent adjustment in your lifestyle

- If you know something is *wrong* emotionally or physically with you or you future spouse, deal with it *now* because the myth that "all we need is love" is just that—a myth!

- A Christian has no business marrying a non-Christian. But realize that the Christian you may be attracted to may have some major physical and/or emotional problems that *will* make your life hell! After all, just because you found that person in church does not mean that they don't have problems. Plus, you may not want to hear this, but the more problematic individuals will never recognize that they have problems; they will think *you* are the one with the problem!

- Remember, ask yourself, "Are we on the same page?"

- Also ask yourself, "Am I a romance novel, whereas s/he is an economics textbook?" In other words, what type of persons do we have mixing here?

- Finally, if your intended spouse has a relative that happens to have a debilitating condition, and it so happens that s/he is the ill person's primary caregiver, buckle up, it's going to be a rough ride ahead! Just think about how many dates you had to break during your courtship due to medical emergencies! You were really ticked off because of those broken dates—what makes you think things will get better "when we get married?" **THINK!**

OK! We're on a roll!

10 Reasons For Marrying A Person That Isn't Honest About Their Emotional Or Physical Issues

1. _____
2. _____
3. _____
4. _____
5. _____
6. _____
7. _____
8. _____
9. _____
10. _____

10 Reasons For Not Marrying A Person That Isn't Honest About Their Emotional Or Physical Issues

1. _____
2. _____
3. _____
4. _____
5. _____
6. _____
7. _____
8. _____
9. _____
10. _____

CHAPTER 6

Marriage: Professional And Vocational Goals—"Hey, What About Me?

I

While it's true that there can be a big difference between personal and professional life, an ill-advised marriage can damage, destroy, or compromise your professional standing. What do I mean? It's simple: a turbulent *home life* can affect your *professional performance* and cause you problems that can take years to resolve. It can even destroy your career! You may then be confused because *you assumed* that your future spouse would automatically understand the importance of what you do, but ask yourself the question, why would you *assume* that? **THINK!**

Sometimes, the person you desire to marry may be "nice," but have an ill-conceived understanding of your professional responsibilities and transfer their fantasies about being able to "help" you into your job responsibilities. Without any understanding of your professional responsibilities, they may confuse the role of *spouse* with *advisor* and cause major problems. Also, if s/he's *unclear* about their role in life, s/he cannot be *clear* about yours; this will cause problems! Remember, the "two shall become one."

II

OK, Lets Take A Plunge Off Of The *Deep* End!

Myths, Vocational Goals, and Marriage (Signs of Possible Trouble)

- S/he "rags" you about how your professional colleagues of the opposite sex are out to "steal you" from him/her.

- Just because s/he's "drop dead gorgeous" or "a hunk" s/he will compliment your professional life. Get real!

- I need to be with ____ because I can get that promotion quicker!

- All of my colleagues will be jealous of me when they see me with ____ on my arm. They will say, it looks like ____'s spouse should be on a magazine cover (after you have been with them for a while you will agree—the *National Enquirer;* stick with them long enough and it will be the *Globe* or *Mad Magazine!*). Stay with them a tad too long, and you may end up on the obituary page before your time.

- I know that s/he is unsaved, chronically unemployed, and generally aimless (at 53 years old?), but *uh-uh-uh*, s/he is sho' nuff *fiiiiiiiiiiiiiioooooooone*! *I* will *save* that person; surely the LORD wouldn't mind that! Plus marriage would make our Biblically compromised relationship "respectable." Also, even though s/he can never seem to celebrate my professional advances—and constantly belittles my achievements—s/he is really a sweetheart. Every time I have to go to a business related activity, s/he screams, "What about me? What about me?" I'm kinda getting tired of all of this, but hey—the fornicating is great, we photograph well together, and my holidays are never spent alone (although after spending Christmas with ____, I dunno!).

- S/he constantly gives you unsolicited advice as to how you can do a better job.

- S/he says, "Your professional advancement is a sign that you are going to leave me, so I will do everything possible to stop you; after all, I'm doing it to *save* our relationship—we're *one*, remember?"

- S/he constantly says that your having to study for your licensing requirements (Bar Exam, Medical Board, Real Estate, Ordination, etc.) is "stupid." The time devoted to studying all of that "stuff should be devoted to *us* (translated *me*)."

- You get an award and you proudly show it to ____. Instead of wanting to celebrate with you, all s/he can scream is, "**What about me? What about me? WHAT ABOUT ME?!**"

- S/he feels threatened, so s/he ridicules your continued progress by calling you "selfish," "narrow minded," a "work-a-holic," and a "sell out to the establishment."

Reality, Professional & Vocational Goals, and Marriage

- We have to be honest with ourselves. Look, if we know that people will sometimes "hook-up" with a person and want to marry them because of fantasies related to how they *look*, what makes us think that the *same* fantasy world in a person's head is not working overtime related to what you *do*? Some people will only date persons in your line of work. They have a *fantasy* in their mind that tells them that if they can just marry a ____, then their life will be complete! I'm sorry to burst your bubble, but, if you were not a ____, s/he may not have given you the time of day.

- Persons that have *no sense* of their own purpose in life *will not understand yours* and in due course will undermine everything surrounding your professional life.

- If you marry a person, and the Lord has not ordained the union, people *will* notice a difference in your performance, dress, temperament, etc.

Hey! I Hate To Burst Your Bubble, But if You Didn't Look A Certain Way Or Have A Certain Job S/He May Not Have Given You The Time Of Day! Many People Get Involved With Others Because They Feel They Need To Present A Certain "Image" To The Public! Is That Your Case? Think About It! (Awww Go On! No One's Looking!)

- They will even chalk it up to your new relationship, they may even start asking you questions like:

    A. Hey, what's happening? All of a sudden your *performance* is *declining*!

    B. You are arriving *late* all the time!

    C. Your *assignments* are *never* on time!

    D. Who is that man/woman that stomped into the restaurant and glared at us while we were in the middle of _____?

    E. Hey, will you please tell _____ I'm your supervisor and not trying to date you?

    F. [They will think to themselves,] "S/he's a pretty level headed person; why would s/he involve him/herself with a person that glared at _____ at the company Christmas party and then screamed, 'I don't care if you are the Regional Vice President; s/he is my man/woman I know you want him/her!' "

When You Get Into A Marital Situation That Does Not Please The Lord, You Will End Up Spending Most Of Your Time Putting Out Fires That Your—A-Hem—"Help-Meet" Sets, Or Maybe It Will Be The Other Way Around! Why Are You Doing This To Yourself? You May Not Want To Admit It Now, But You Aren't Getting Very Much Work Done! THINK!

Stick With Me! No Time To Quit Now!

THINK!

- "Hooking up" with the wrong person *will* have a detrimental effect upon your life and career! You could begin to do some of the following:

    A. Work extra hours, *not* because you need to, but because you *want to avoid* the fire breathing, immature dragon you have involved yourself with. This can lead to more escapist, as well as dangerous activities, like drug and/or alcohol abuse, extra-marital affairs, etc.

    B. If you make the humongous mistake of marrying this person, you will end up turning down promotions because your advancement would be a threat to _____.

    C. Also, if you marry this person, you will be afraid to accept a transfer to a higher paying position with more responsibility, because s/he has a tendency to "clown" you in private, and sadly enough, in public. At least at this level, you can kind of keep a "lid" on him/her—

but you and I both know it will get worse if you get promoted and have an assignment with a high profile!

D. If you take such a foolish step, you will waste valuable time and energy dealing with a person that may "go off" at any moment (**Proverbs 12:16, 25, 15:13**).

III

The Bible Speaks To Our Professional/Vocational Goals

When the Scriptures speak to our professional and vocational goals, it is then that it relates to our sense of "**CALLING**." Too bad we only think of "**CALLING**" as *preaching*. God **CALLS** us to what ever our level of interest/competence happens to be. Why shouldn't He? After all, He created us. He also placed within us our interests and competence! God is the one that puts those abilities and interests into our mind. He also gives us the ability to function within our positions. The key to a fruitful life is committing our life totally to the LORD (**Proverbs 16:1**).

Biblical Examples Of Persons Being "Called"

- Abraham was *called* (**Genesis 12:1-3, 15, 17**) to be faithful to God, but *never stopped* being a nomadic wanderer (**Genesis 12: 10-20, 13:1-13**).

- We are all *called* to be a nation of priests (**1 Peter 2:9-10**)! To limit this calling to "preaching" is ridiculous!

- We are *called* to function, under the leadership of the Holy Spirit (**Romans 8:1-17**), at our peak, so as not to bring *shame* (**Romans 2:17-24**) upon the Gospel, the Lord, or the Church Family (**2 Thessalonians 3:6-14, 1 Peter 3: 8-17**).

- How can you be faithful to your *calling* if you have "hell at home (**Proverbs 11:29, 12:4, 20:13, 21:9, 19, and 27: 15-16**)?"

- How can you make intelligent and Godly decisions at work when you have "hooked up" with a carnal and/or silly, immature as well as manipulative person, that you have a tendency to "give in to" for the "sake of peace," even when their suggestions are foolish (**Genesis 16:1-4**)? Even if s/he forgets that it was not your suggestion, s/he will blame you when the results if the suggestion do not go in a favorable direction (**Genesis 16:5-6**)! Relationships such as these have a tendency to sap energy and can bring your life to a screeching halt.

IV

Suggested Process

- You need to take a long hard look at your personal and professional goals. Ask some questions.

  A. Will your *proposed spouse* enhance your professional life, or rip it to shreds? Will *you* enhance that person's life, or will you tear it to shreds?

  B. Are you picking up signals that all may not be right in terms of your professional life relative to ____? And vice versa?

  C. Are you picking up negative signals and yet you don't want to "let go" because s/he has "so much potential, and I know that every thing will work out 'cause I have faith, as soon as I slip a ring on _____'s finger, everything will be ok!" Come on, who are you kidding? Who died and appointed you God anyway?

  D. Check out a qualified emotional health professional and get a grip on your "need" to self-destruct. Remember, the "two shall become one."

E. The relationship may be worth salvaging if the two of you can also go into therapy and consult with a career counselor. An introduction, where permissible, to what you do professionally and vice versa should be done; both parties should know what it takes for the other to function in their chosen line of work. After all, you have invested lots of money, time, studying, etc., in terms of your chosen field. Are you going to let a marriage—unsanctioned by the Lord—rip it to pieces? *THINK* about it!

Resources

Letitia Baldrige's *New Complete Guide to Executive Manners*. New York: Charles Scribner's Sons, 1993.

Richard Nelson Bolles' *The 1999 What Color is Your Parachute? A Practical Manual for Job-Hunters and Career-Changers*. Berkeley, CA: Ten Speed Press, 1999. Note: Bolles has an extensive listing of career counselors located in the USA and overseas. For the 1999 edition, you will find it starts on page 318.

Epilogue
For
Some Thoughts for the Journey to Cana

Perhaps one of the biggest challenges to living a coherent life under God, through Jesus Christ, is being able to surrender our lives to the Master for safe keeping.

Why don't we do it? Whether it's in marriage, professional advancement, financial planning, or even meeting basic responsibilities such as parenting, paying bills when due, or keeping a roof over our heads, in many cases, we come up short and turn our day-to-day lives into blazing infernos. The excuses for "hell on earth" existences are somewhat well worn and familiar:

- "Well, I was always taught..."
- "Well, I was never taught..."
- "I never knew that it would turn out this way..."

Now, Come Up With Some Of Your Own—Don't Be Chicken, It Will Be Our Little Secret!

- _____
- _____
- _____
- _____
- _____
- _____

As you can see, the list can be endless. The results of entering into such close relationships as marriage, and in due course "self-destructing," can be devastating. Also, even if our parents never taught us certain things, it thrusts our *marital partners* into trying to do what the *parents* should have done—namely, raising you! Make no mistake—and it's a hard pill to swallow—it's tough to find out that you married a four-year-old that masqueraded as an adult. The trouble and hassle produced by immaturity and unwise decisions can destroy us, whether we like it or not!

There's Nothing Worse Than Thinking That You Are Marrying An Adult, But Instead, You Find A Toddler Masquerading As A Grown-up! After A While It Stops Being "Cute" And Becomes Down Right Depressing!

We can holler, scream, threaten, make excuses, bully, blackmail, "lay guilt trips," and extort one another through a hellish relationship, but society is swift to punish us, regardless as to the fact that we were "never taught" basic survival skills!

Remember:

- Your local utility company couldn't care less that you thought that it was joking—and didn't pay your bill because you wanted to "treat" yourself to a _____!

- Landlords can and will evict you if destroy their property.

- You will always be at the mercy of others if your debts constantly exceed your income.

- An unsanctioned marriage can destroy in a few minutes what may have taken someone years to build.

- The fact that you felt "distant" from your mother is no reason to attempt to find "mommy" or "daddy" in a potential spouse!

- Marriage will not fix all of your problems!

- The District Attorney takes a dim view of the fact that you write checks, with nothing in the bank. S/he doesn't care whether your "mommy" or "daddy" never told you how to balance a checkbook, and you keep writing checks!

- You will bounce from job to job and never advance if you were never taught such basic skills. A few of those basic skills are for example: showing up on time, doing the work assigned, not going AWOL "'cause I needed a break," and that you feel that to work means that you have "sold out to the establishment." This attitude will destroy, or at least make difficult, the life of your future spouse!

Remember, The "Two Shall Become One!"

Within the context of a marriage, what you *do does matter*! If you want to do it "solo" or have "unfinished business" with your parents, children, or "ex", becoming "one" with someone else may not be the best thing for you right now.

Finally, remember that the only role models worthy of imitating, as far as marriage commitments are those found in the Bible (**Exodus 20:1-4, Hosea 1, Isaiah 54:1-6, Ephesians 5:21-32, and Revelation 21:2-9, 22:17**). Any other role model is strictly of the **WORLD**—which includes friends and relatives, no matter how dear they are to you!

Reference Scriptures:

- You know you are not ready for the "grown up" world, if you reject the Scripture **(Proverbs 9:7)**.

- You know that you are not ready for the "grown up" world, if you "qualify" the Word—just take the Bible at face value! Don't say, "I know what the Bible says—but *my* case is different **(Genesis 3:1-7)**."

- You know you are not ready for the "grown up" world, if you refuse to believe that "fat meat is greasy" **(Proverbs 11:29, 12:4, 15, 13:13, 18, 14:1, 17:12)**.

You Are Not Ready For A "Grown Up" Commitment Like Marriage If You...

A. Rush headlong to the altar without doing what the Master commanded. After all, didn't He order us to "count up the costs" **(Luke 14:31)**?

B. Are in a dysfunctional marriage/situation and refuse to follow the advice of the Scripture and seek out Wisdom **(Proverbs 1:20-33)**. If we refuse Wisdom, the Bible has but one word for us: *"FOOL"* **(Proverbs**

18:6-7), and are therefore a danger to ourselves as well as everyone around us (**Proverbs 17:12**).

However, all is not lost! Within the Bible, there is *healing* and *hope* (**Isaiah 55, James 1:5-8 and 1 John 1:9-10**)! Just remember one thing as you journey to Cana—not only is it important for our Master to meet us at Cana, but through the engagement process—the journey to Cana, it's a good idea to have Him lead you!

www.ingramcontent.com/pod-product-compliance
Lightning Source LLC
Chambersburg PA
CBHW050835160426
43192CB00010B/2042